THE BACK OF THE NAPKIN

THE BACK
OF
THE NAPKIN

Solving Problems
and Selling Ideas with Pictures

DAN ROAM

Portfolio

PORTFOLIO
Published by the Penguin Group
Penguin Group (USA) Inc., 375 Hudson Street, New York, New York 10014, U.S.A. • Penguin Group (Canada), 90 Eglinton Avenue East, Suite 700, Toronto, Ontario, Canada M4P 2Y3 (a division of Pearson Penguin Canada Inc.) • Penguin Books Ltd, 80 Strand, London WC2R 0RL, England • Penguin Ireland, 25 St. Stephen's Green, Dublin 2, Ireland (a division of Penguin Books Ltd) • Penguin Books Australia Ltd, 250 Camberwell Road, Camberwell, Victoria 3124, Australia (a division of Pearson Australia Group Pty Ltd) • Penguin Books India Pvt Ltd, 11 Community Centre, Panchsheel Park, New Delhi–110 017, India • Penguin Group (NZ), 67 Apollo Drive, Rosedale, North Shore 0632, New Zealand (a division of Pearson New Zealand Ltd) • Penguin Books (South Africa) (Pty) Ltd, 24 Sturdee Avenue, Rosebank, Johannesburg 2196, South Africa

Penguin Books Ltd, Registered Offices:
80 Strand, London WC2R 0RL, England

First published in 2008 by Portfolio,
a member of Penguin Group (USA) Inc.

10   9   8

Copyright © Digital Roam, Inc., 2008
All rights reserved

Illustrations by the author

Library of Congress Cataloging-in-Publication Data

Roam, Dan.
The back of the napkin : solving problems and selling ideas with pictures / Dan Roam.
p.   cm.
ISBN 978-1-59184-199-9
1. Problem solving—Audio-visual aids.   2. Management—Audio-visual aids.   3. Visualization.
4. Creative ability in business.   I. Title.

HD30.29.R625 2008
658.4'03—dc22   2007029023

Printed in the United States of America
Set in Dante MT with Felt Tip and Divine
Designed by Daniel Lagin

Without limiting the rights under copyright reserved above, no part of this publication may be reproduced, stored in or introduced into a retrieval system, or transmitted, in any form or by any means (electronic, mechanical, photocopying, recording or otherwise), without the prior written permission of both the copyright owner and the above publisher of this book.

The scanning, uploading, and distribution of this book via the Internet or via any other means without the permission of the publisher is illegal and punishable by law. Please purchase only authorized electronic editions and do not participate in or encourage electronic piracy of copyrightable materials. Your support of the author's rights is appreciated.

For Isabelle.

You saw this book coming long before I did,
and you saw it through in every way. Now that's love.

CONTENTS

Part III: Developing Ideas
The Visual Thinking MBA: Putting Visual Thinking to Work

Part IV: Selling Ideas
It's Showtime

THE BACK
OF
THE NAPKIN

PART 1
INTRODUCTIONS

Anytime, Anyone, Anywhere:
Solving Problems with Pictures

CHAPTER 1

A WHOLE NEW WAY OF LOOKING AT BUSINESS

What's the most daunting business problem you can picture? Is it global and expansive, or small and personal? Is it political, technical, or emotional? Is it about money, process, or people? Is it rooted in the day-to-day operations of your company, or is it floating high off in the conceptual ether? Is the problem you see one you know well, or one you've never looked at before?

I'll bet you can come up with a problem that meets every one of these criteria. I know I can: managing businesses in San Francisco, Moscow, Zurich, and New York, I've dealt with problems across this spectrum myself—and seen many more dealt with by colleagues, bosses, employees, and clients. It's true: The heart of business is the art of problem solving.

What if there was a way to more quickly look at problems, more intuitively understand them, more confidently address them, and more rapidly convey to others what we've discovered? What if there was a way to make business problem solving more efficient, more effective, and—as much as I hate to say it—perhaps even a bit more *fun*? There is. It's called visual thinking, and it's what this book is all about: solving problems with pictures.

Here's my elevator pitch:

> *Visual thinking means taking advantage of our innate ability to see—both with our eyes and with our mind's eye—in order to discover ideas that are otherwise invisible, develop those ideas quickly and intuitively, and then share those ideas with other people in a way that they simply "get."*

That's it. Welcome to a whole new way of looking at business.

"I'm Not a Visual Person"

Before I quickly share with you an overview of this book, let me start with the most important idea of all: Solving problems with pictures has nothing to do with artistic training or talent. That's right—*nothing*. I emphasize this because every time I'm invited to help a company solve a problem with pictures or talk to a group of businesspeople about visual thinking, somebody always says, "Wait. This isn't for me—I'm not a visual person."

To which I say, "OK, that's fine, but let me put it this way: If you were able to walk into this room this morning without falling down, I guarantee that you're enough of a visual person to understand everything that we're going to talk about and to get something useful out of it."

In fact (for lots of reasons we'll explore throughout this book), the people who start out by saying, "I can't draw, but . . . ," almost always end up creating some of the most insightful pictures. So if you're not convinced of your drawing skills, please don't put this book down yet. Instead, jump straight to page 22—if you can draw the box, arrow, and stick figure you'll find there, this book is for you.

Visual Thinking in Four Lessons

Here's how this book works. *The Back of the Napkin* is divided into four parts—this introduction and then one part each for *discovering* ideas, *developing* ideas, and *selling* ideas, all using nothing but our eyes, our mind's eye, our hands, a pen, and a scrap of paper. (Whiteboards are good, too.)

In this introduction, we're going to define which *problems* we're talking about (all of them), which *pictures* we're talking about (very simple ones), and *who* can do this (all of us). We'll then talk about how—though our innate visual thinking skills vary—we can all do this, and we'll even run through a short checklist to help us better understand what kind of visual thinkers we are. Then, we'll talk about how simple the process of visual thinking really is, and how we already know how to do every step.

In part II, Discovering Ideas, we'll run through the foundations of good visual thinking: learning how to *look better,* how to *see sharper,* and how to *imagine further.* Then we'll familiarize ourselves with the basic tool kit of visual thinking: the SQVID (which forces our brain into visual action whether we want it to or not), the <6><6> framework (which helps us map what we've seen to what we want to show), and then the Visual Thinking Codex (which provides a cheat sheet for starting any picture we can think up).

In part III, Developing Ideas, we're going to take a page from a typical MBA program and walk step-by-step through a business case study—and we're going to *draw* on that page. By the time we're done, we'll have road-tested the six fundamental frameworks of problem-solving pictures—and saved a business along the way.

Finally, we'll come to the last part, Selling Ideas, where we'll pull everything together to create and deliver a sales presentation that requires no computers, no software, no projector, and no color handouts—just us, our client, a big whiteboard, and a lot of well-focused ideas.

Where All This Came from: English Breakfast (aka How Visual Thinking Saved My Bacon)

When I asked you a moment ago to conjure up the most daunting business problem you could, I was myself thinking of a specific challenge that I faced several years ago, an incident that prompted me to start thinking in detail about everything that you'll find in this book.

Perhaps you've been in a similar situation: Asked at the last moment to cover for a colleague, you say yes only to realize that you've stepped into your worst nightmare. In this case, my colleague had to leave the office on a medical emergency and pleaded with me to cover for a speech he had to deliver the following day. I said yes, only to learn later that the speech was to take place in Sheffield, England (we were in New York) to an audience of educational experts appointed by the then-new British prime minister, Tony Blair. My colleague hadn't told me what the topic was—something about the Internet—or where his materials (if there were any) were buried.

So I found myself the next morning on a train departing from London's St. Pancras Station for Sheffield, jet-lagged from a transatlantic flight, surrounded by a group of British colleagues I'd never met before, all thanking me profusely for coming to "save their sales pitch." Save the pitch? I didn't even know what time it was.

But then came along a most marvelous discovery: English breakfast on British Rail. As the train sped through the British Midlands, white-jacketed waiters served us a feast: scrambled eggs, poached eggs, boiled potatoes, fried potatoes, potato pancakes, blood sausages, white sausages, grilled sausages, white sauce, and Tabasco; toast, rolls, rye bread, rice pudding; coffee, tea, milk, orange juice, apricot juice, and ice water. It was a revelation.

But by the time we'd made it through breakfast, I was feeling human again. That's when Freddie (the British team leader) asked me to walk him through my PowerPoint presentation. Wait—*my* PowerPoint presentation? But I didn't have a presentation, I explained; I wasn't even sure what we were supposed to be talking about.

"Uh . . . the role of the Internet in American education," Freddie said as a look of panic crossed his face. "You do know something about that, don't you?" he pleaded.

"Actually . . . no," I replied, as I turned to the window and contemplated how best to jump off the train. But then another idea began to resolve itself in my mind's eye, so I pulled a pen from my suit pocket and grabbed a stack of napkins from the table.

"I don't know much about educational Web sites specifically, but I do know a lot about creating communications-oriented Web sites," I said, pen poised over napkin. "Can I show you something that your education experts might find interesting? I have an idea."

Before Freddie could answer, my pen was already moving. And this is what I drew: a circle with the word "brand" in the middle of it.

"You see, Freddie," I said, "lots of people these days are very confused about how to create a useful Web site—and I imagine the same is true of our audience today. But the way I think about it, there are really only three things that we need to worry about. The first is the brand itself. The other two are the content and the function." I drew in two more circles and labeled them appropriately, then continued. "If we can determine what to put in these three circles, then we can build any site to serve any audience, including your educators.

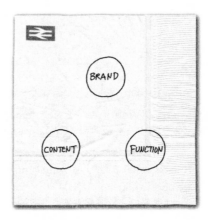

"The question is, How do we know what these three should contain? The answer is this." I drew a little smiley face next to each circle and wrote a caption for each. "What people want to DO (or what we want them to do) determines *function;* what people want to KNOW (or what we want them to know) determines *content;* and what we want them to REMEMBER determines the *brand.*

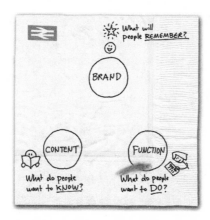

"We can determine all these things through our client's business vision, market studies, and basic educational research. We don't have to know all these answers today; the point of this picture is that it gives us a good starting point for knowing *who* and *what* we should be looking for."

Next I drew in three more smiley faces and captions, this time connecting the three circles together. "If our research tells us *what* to put in those three circles, then it's our own Web site team who will create it. Our engineers build the functional components; our writers define, write, and edit the content; and our designers create an experience that will be memorable.

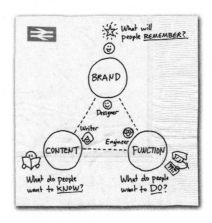

"Simple as it seems, that's pretty much it."
I then summarized the napkin with a title and a key.

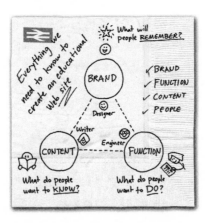

"What do you think, Freddie? Could I walk our audience through something like that?" My napkin wasn't beautiful by any stretch, but it struck me as clear, comprehensive, and comprehensible—and simple as it was, it gave me about a dozen starting places to talk in more detail about any aspect of creating a useful Web site.

Freddie tore the napkin out of my hands. "That's brilliant! That's not part of our presentation—that's the whole thing! Think about who we're talking to." Freddie explained. "Our audience is a group of highly educated government bureaucrats, all new to the Internet. A lot of public money is going to be spent on their online education project, and their necks are on the line. Their greatest concern is that there is a solid framework under their feet to give them confidence to move forward. Your napkin provides the structure they're looking for. This is perfect"—Freddie leaned back and looked at me—"but do you think you can talk about it for forty-five minutes?"

"We'll find out soon enough," I replied.

It turns out that the classic lecture halls of Sheffield University have the biggest blackboards I'd ever seen. So I redrew the napkin step-by-step before the audience of fifty experts, walking them through it just as I had with Freddie over breakfast. We didn't just talk about it for forty-five minutes; they so enjoyed the process that we ended up talking for nearly two hours. Freddie's team won the engagement, and thus began the longest-running project of the London office.

And me? Sharing that simple napkin in that grand university hall was my watershed moment in understanding the power of pictures. I thought about all the problems that that simple napkin sketch had helped solve: First, simply by drawing it, I had clarified in my own mind a previously vague idea. Second, I was able to create the picture almost instantly, without the need to rely on any technology other than paper and pen. Third, I was able to share the picture with my audiences in an open way that invited comments and inspired discussion. Finally, speaking directly from the picture meant I could focus on any topic without having to rely on notes, bullet points, or a written script.

The lesson for me was clear. We can use the simplicity and immediacy of pictures to discover and clarify our own ideas, and use those same pictures to clarify our ideas for other people, helping them discover something new for themselves along the way.

After the eye-opening success of that English breakfast, I returned home inspired to learn all I could about the use of pictures as a problem-solving approach. Back in

New York, I focused my attention on seeing how far I could push the use of images in discovering, developing, and sharing business ideas. I read everything I could find about business visualization, I attended workshops led by the gurus of information visualization, and I searched for and collected all the visual explanations I could find in the business press.

Two things surprised me. First, I was shocked at how few materials I could find on visual thinking as a problem-solving approach—and of those, how few offered practical advice for the day-to-day world of business—and second, what initially appeared to be a wildly divergent set of materials in fact masked a small set of common themes. This last point struck me as particularly compelling. If visual thinking could usefully be broken down into a set of common tools, perhaps it could become a recognized way of approaching all sorts of business challenges, from idea discovery to concept development to communications to sales.

I also realized that the best way to test these common tools was to put them into practice on real-world business consulting and sales assignments. So from that point on, I decided that wherever I *could* use a picture in my job, I *would*. The rest of this book is about what happened next.

CHAPTER 2

WHICH PROBLEMS, WHICH PICTURES, AND WHO IS "WE"?

What I Hope You Get from This Book

In a single ten-week period earlier this year, I worked with four very different companies—Google, eBay, Wells Fargo, and Peet's Coffee and Tea—to help out on four very different business challenges: defining a business strategy, implementing a new product, designing a technology platform, and launching a new sales initiative. On the surface, the four companies and their four problems had nothing in common: searching, selling, banking, and brewing. Normally, a different problem-solving approach would be required for each.

But just below the surface, all shared something in common: The problems were hard to see and their solutions were nearly invisible. That's where visual thinking came in: Any problem can be made clearer with a picture, and any picture can be created using the same set of tools and rules.

Here's what I hope you get from this book—a new way of looking at problems and a new way of seeing solutions. I want you to be able to read this book in the time it takes to fly coast to coast, step into your conference room, auditorium, or cubicle the next day, and immediately start solving problems with pictures.

Problems? What Problems?

To this day, when I hear myself say, "We can solve problems with pictures," three questions immediately jump to mind: first, What problems?; second, What pictures?; and third, Who is "we"?

Let's start with the problems. What kinds can be solved with pictures? The answer is almost all of them. Because pictures can represent complex concepts and summarize vast sets of information in ways that are easy for us to see and understand, they are useful for clarifying and resolving problems of all sorts: business issues, political deadlocks, technical complexities, organizational dilemmas, scheduling conflicts, even personal challenges.

Since I am a businessperson and work with other businesspeople, the problems that I usually focus on are business related: getting teams of people to understand how a system works and where they fit into that system, helping a decision maker clarify his or her own thinking and improve the ways she or he conveys ideas to others, understanding a market and the potential impact that changes to a product may have on it.

Because these problems typically involve lots of money and have an impact on the work of so many people—and because understanding their critical nuances typically takes years of study and experience—it is easy to consider these problems as being unique to business. But they're really not. For the purposes of introducing visual thinking, it's much more illuminating to consider these problems as representative of a broader set of common challenges that we all face every day, in business and in life.

Looking at the bigger picture, I clump most problems into the following basic (and familiar) set of categories.

1. *Who* and *what* problems. Challenges that relate to things, people, and roles.

- What is going on around me, and where do I fit in?
- Who is in charge and who else is involved? Where does responsibility lie?

2. *How much* problems. Challenges that involve measuring and counting.

- Do we have enough of X to last as long as we need?
- How much of X do we need to keep going? If we increase this over here, can we decrease that over there?

3. *When* problems. Challenges that relate to scheduling and timing.

- What comes first, and what comes next?
- We've got a lot of things to do: When are we going to do them all?

4. *Where* problems. Challenges that relate to direction and how things fit together.

- Where are we going now? Are we headed in the right direction, or should we be moving elsewhere?
- How do all these pieces fit together? What's most important and what matters less?

5. *How* problems. Challenges that relate to how things influence one another.

- What will happen if we do this? What about that?
- Can we alter the outcomes of a situation by altering our actions?

6. *Why* problems. Challenges that relate to seeing the big picture.

- What are we really doing, and why? Is it the right thing, or should we be doing something different?
- If we need to change, what are our options? How can we decide which of those options are best?

Over the years, I've seen or created pictures that helped solve problems in all six categories. In fact, because this simple 6 W's model covers just about every problem that I can recall working on, we're going to see it time and again throughout this book. Some time ago, early in my initial push toward visual problem solving, I even developed a little mantra about it: "Any problem can be helped with a picture." I said it so often that I drove my colleagues crazy, especially on projects such as this next one.

PROBLEM EXAMPLE NUMBER ONE:
DAPHNE AND THE INFORMATION OVERLOAD

One day a couple years after my trip to London, our consulting company received a call from a potential client. The caller—let's call her Daphne*—was the vice president of communications at a large publishing company, and Daphne was having an identity crisis. Her company, a $10 billion-a-year conglomerate that provided business information to professionals around the globe, had just received frighteningly low marks in an industry survey. It wasn't that the professionals surveyed thought badly of the company, the problem was that despite the company's size, nobody had ever heard of it.

This wasn't just a perception problem; this lack of recognition posed an even bigger financial problem. The company was planning to list on the New York Stock Exchange in a couple years, and if nobody knew who they were, nobody would buy their stock. What Daphne needed was a way to increase recognition of the company's name among investors, and she needed to think strategically about it. If she was going to spend millions of dollars promoting the company's brand, she'd better have a rock-solid plan behind her and a crystal-clear vision ahead. Even with the *when* nailed down (two years), the *where* pinpointed (the United States, especially New York), and the *why* clear (raise investor awareness), Daphne still had to answer the *who*, *what*, *how* questions.

In order to better understand what investors and clients knew about her company and its competitors, Daphne hired a brand survey firm to go around the world and find out.

---

* All characters, companies, and projects in this book are real, but I have changed most of the personal names.

Over a three-month period, the survey firm completed face-to-face interviews with hundreds of business decision makers and talked on the phone with hundreds more. It was a large and expensive undertaking and, as hoped, delivered an enormous amount of data.

The problem was, it delivered too much, and that's why Daphne was calling us. Her goal wasn't to know *everything* in the world about publishing; it was to know the *right things* to help her define her plan and vision. In the end, what Daphne most wanted was for us to help her see what the data really showed.

Daphne e-mailed us all the brand survey documents. There were dozens, each thicker and more detailed than the next. Even the file called "executive summary" was sixty pages long, jam-packed with more information than we could really make sense of in the two weeks that Daphne had given us. This is just one section of one document that Daphne passed on to us.

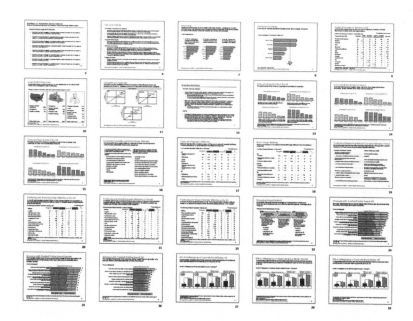

It was a bullet-point and bar-chart bonanza. We spent our first several days just trying to find what mattered most—while making sure not to miss any small yet critical detail. We were learning a lot, but we were becoming saturated with details at the expense of the big picture. The sad thing was that there was a lot of great information and insight there; it was just buried so deeply and spread so widely that nobody could find it.

So we broke everything we could into one or more of the six "problem categories" and then scoured through, mapping what we found onto paper:

1. **The *who/what:*** The list of competitors, the industries they served, and the products they offered.

2. **The *how much:*** The size of each competitor based on total revenue and revenue per industry.

3. **The *when:*** The two years for which we had good sales and revenue data.

4. **The *where:*** The industries each competitor served.

Then we plotted on top of all that:

5. **The *how:*** How did the brand survey findings (brand recognition) map to all these factors?

What emerged was a single picture that summarized all the data, showing the most important insight of all:

6. **The *why:*** When looking at the chart, Daphne was able to finally see why her company was unknown to her clients, and why a positive change was possible.

This is the picture we came up with.

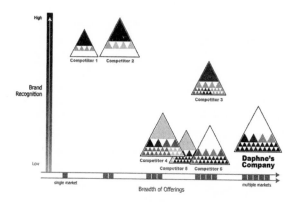

This single image summarized everything presented in the hundreds of pages of data we'd been given. Admittedly, it's not a chart that someone can "get" the first moment he or she looks at it, but then it didn't need to be. As a visual executive summary of hundreds of data points, it was intended to be accompanied by a few minutes of explanation (and in the last chapter of this book, we'll talk about why that's a *good* thing). Compared to the impenetrable wall of survey data, this picture served Daphne well, both as the summary of what she had found in her global study and as her introduction to where she wanted to take the brand.

When Daphne presented it to her CEO, he spent thirty minutes discussing what he saw in the chart, and then asked to have a framed copy to hang behind his desk so that he could share it with anyone who asked him about the company's present and future market position. Two years later, the company listed successfully on the New York Stock Exchange, and to this day the chart still hangs in the CEO's office.

Pictures? What Pictures?

Before moving on, I want to point out two additional things about Daphne's picture. First, it was drawn on a computer using an expensive software program. You can tell because all the lines are straight, it has many precise levels of color shading, the shapes are mathematically perfect, and the typeface is clean and readable. Second, it is the only picture in this book drawn on a computer. I like to show this chart up front because it illustrates what can be created once we've got down the basics of visual thinking. But now that we've seen it, I'd like to forget all about it. Here's why: The basics of visual thinking have nothing to do with creating charts on a computer. Visual thinking is learning to think with our eyes, and it doesn't require any advanced technology at all.

There are really only three tools that we'll need to become great at solving problems with pictures: our eyes, our mind's eye, and a little hand-eye coordination. I call these our "built-in" visual thinking tools:

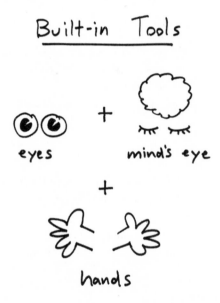

With just these available, we've got everything we need to get started. There are also a few accessories that will help.

Accessories

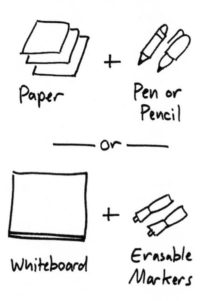

Paper + Pen or Pencil

— or —

Whiteboard + Erasable Markers

The reason we won't need computer software or sophisticated data-plotting programs is because every picture we're going to make will be composed of just a few simple pieces, all of which we should already be able to get down on paper. If you can scrawl out the following (regardless of how ugly you find your results), you're guaranteed to become a better visual thinker.

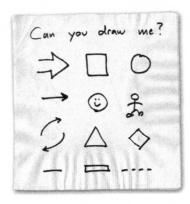

Throughout this book, the pictures we'll be looking at and creating include charts, diagrams, schematics, flowcharts, tables, maps, *x-y* plots, concept models, network models, and many other kinds of visuals, and not one of them will require anything more than these pieces.

As a little warm-up exercise, pick up your pen and paper, and try your hand at sketching out the basics.

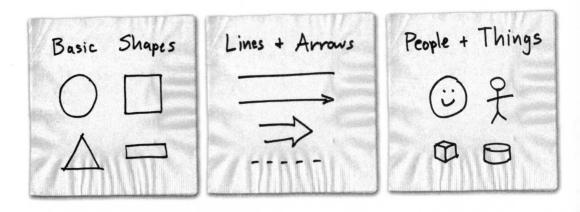

If you've used a software presentation tool (PowerPoint, Keynote, Star Office, etc.) in the past, you might recognize the above as part of the "drawing tools palette." There's a reason they appear so frequently: These few shapes are the core alphabet of visual thinking. In the same way that written languages use a limited number of symbols to represent thousands of sounds and words, combinations of these symbols can create millions of powerful pictures.

Take a look at the following summary of pictures that appear in this book, and see if you can find these basics throughout. Although every one of the pictures tells a different story, they are all made up of the same pieces. When you feel comfortable sketching out what's above, you can make any of what's on the next page.

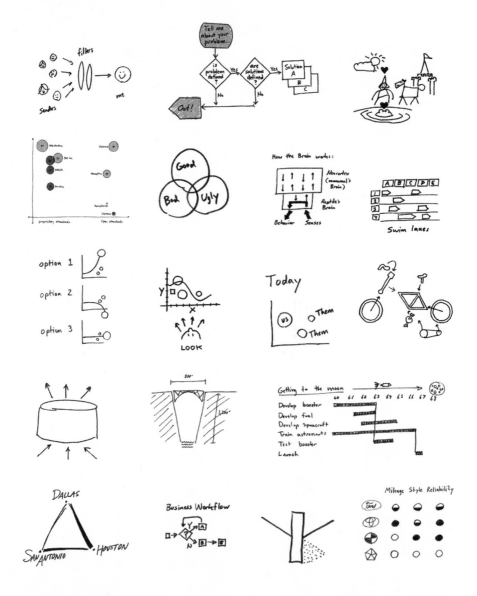

The Hand Is Mightier Than the Mouse

Regardless of the names we'll eventually give them (and we are going to give them all names), these are the kinds of pictures this book is about. They can all be drawn by hand, and it's important, especially as we get started, that we *do* learn to make them by hand. Partly it is a question of visual confidence: The more we can rely on our three "built-in" visual thinking tools (eyes, mind's eye, hand-eye coordination), the more we'll discover about our innate visual thinking abilities.

This reliance on our built-in tools will also pay off when it comes time to share our pictures with others:

1. **People like seeing other people's pictures.** In most presentation situations, audiences respond better to hand-drawn images (however crudely drawn) than to polished graphics. The spontaneity and roughness of hand-drawn pictures make them less intimidating and more inviting—and nothing makes an image (even a complex image) clearer than seeing it drawn out step-by-step.

2. **Hand-sketched images are quick to create and easy to change.** As we'll see, thinking with pictures is fluid, and visual trial and error happens all the time. It is rare that the picture we end up with is exactly what we had in mind when we began, so being able to go back and make changes is important.

3. **Computers make it too easy to draw the wrong thing.** Most software programs used for creating pictures come with several built-in chart-making functions. That's great, assuming we know which type of chart is most useful in making our point . . . an assumption that is almost always incorrect.

The most important reason to rely on our built-in tools is because in the end, visual thinking isn't about how polished our presentations are, it is in how comfortable we are in thinking with our eyes.

Black Pen, Yellow Pen, Red Pen: Who Is "We"?

Whenever I tell people that I help solve business problems with pictures, they react in one of three ways. They say, "Cool! Can you show me how?" Or "Sounds interesting . . . but does that really work?" Or "Forget it. I'm not a visual person."

"Hand me the pen!"

"I can't draw, but..."

"I'm not visual."

Black Pen   Yellow Pen (Highlighter)   Red Pen

There are three kinds of visual thinkers: people who can't wait to start drawing (the Black Pen people), those who are happy to add to someone else's work (the Yellow highlighters), and those who question it all—right up to the moment they pick up the red pen and redraw it all.

The first group is the "Hand me the pen" people. In my highly unscientific survey of business meetings I've attended, these people typically represent about a quarter of the attendees. I call them the Black Pen people because they show no hesitation in putting the first bold marks on an empty page. They come across as immediate believers in the power of pictures as a problem-solving tool, and have little concern about their drawing skills—regardless of how primitive their illustrations may turn out to be. These people jump at the chance to approach the whiteboard and draw images to describe what they're thinking. They enjoy identifying visual metaphors and analogies for their ideas, and show great confidence in drawing simple images, both to summarize their ideas and then help work through those ideas.

The second group is the "I can't draw, but . . ." people, otherwise known as the Yellow Pen people (or highlighters) because they're often very good at identifying the most important or interesting aspects of what someone else has drawn. This group usually makes up about half of the meeting population. These are the people who are happy to watch someone else working at the whiteboard—and after a few minutes will begin to make insightful comments—but who need to be gently prodded to stand and approach the board in order to add to it. Once at the board and with pen tentatively in hand, they always begin by saying, "I can't draw, but . . . ," and then proceed to create conceptual masterworks. These people tend to be more verbal, usually incorporate more words and labels into their sketches, and are more likely to make comparisons to ideas that require supporting verbal descriptions.

The last group I call the "I'm not visual" or Red Pen people. Representing the last quarter of the meeting population, these people are least comfortable with the use of pictures in a business context . . . at least at first. They tend to be quiet while others are sketching away, and when they can be coaxed to comment, most often initially suggest a minor correction of something already there. But that's usually a cover. Quite often, the Red Pens have the most detailed grasp of the problem at hand—they just need to be coaxed into sharing it. The Red Pens think of themselves as quantitatively oriented—almost mathematical—but once prompted will provide deep background explanations through persuasive speaking. But watch out: When many images and ideas have been captured on the whiteboard, the Red Pen people will finally take a deep breath, reluctantly pick up the pen, and move to the board . . . where they redraw everything, often coming up with the clearest picture of them all.

An interesting note on these three groups is that they don't correlate to age, education, background, job role, or title. I've worked with a CEO at a global consulting company who draws everything out on sheets of tabloid paper as his way of thinking through a problem and sharing his ideas with his team, and I've also worked with another CEO who is among the most charismatic and spontaneous public speakers I've ever met, but who quakes at the idea of approaching a whiteboard. One of my frequent collaborators is a Johns Hopkins–trained MD who creates miraculous visual descriptions of even complex concepts, and I've worked with hard-core "geek" software engineers who couldn't wait to start drawing.

Your Pen Is What Color?

Before we go on, let's take a moment to see if we can't identify which pen color you prefer. As you imagine participating in a business meeting or group problem-solving setting, how do you see yourself in one of these three "colored pen" groups? Does your approach change depending on the type of problem you're looking at, the people around you, or whether you're in a group or working alone?

"WHICH COLOR IS YOUR PEN?" SELF-ASSESSMENT

Select the single best answer for each of the situations below:

I'm in a brainstorming session in a conference room that has a big whiteboard. I want to:

1. Go to the board, pick up a pen, and start drawing circles and boxes.
2. Try to decipher whatever is already written on the board.
3. Go to the board and start writing categorized lists.
4. Add a little clarification to what's already up there, to make it clearer.
5. "Forget the whiteboard. Come on here, people, we've got work to do!"
6. I hate brainstorming sessions.

Someone hands me a complex, multipage spreadsheet table printout. I first:

1. Glaze over, put it down, and hope it will go away.
2. Flip through the pages letting my eye wander across all those numbers to see if something interesting—anything—pops up.
3. Read across the top of the columns or down each row in order, looking to identify the categories.
4. Select a row and column at random and follow them to the data cell, then look for similar (or different) data results in other cells.

5. Look for the largest or smallest values I can find, then trace them back to identify their categories.

6. Flip back and forth between sheets and zero in on the important patterns that I saw right away.

Someone hands me a pen and asks me to sketch out a particular idea. I:

1. Ask for more pens, preferably in at least three colors.

2. Just start sketching and see what emerges.

3. Say, "I can't draw but . . . ," and then make a horrible stick figure.

4. Start by writing a few words, then putting boxes around them.

5. Put the pen on the table and start talking.

6. Say, "No, thanks, I can't draw," and leave it at that.

On my way home from a big conference, I run into a colleague at the airport bar, and he or she asks me to explain more precisely what my company does. I:

1. Grab a napkin and ask the bartender for a pen.

2. Pick up three packs of Sweet'N Low, lay them on the bar, and say, "OK, this is me. . . ."

3. Pull up a page from my PowerPoint—a really good page—and start describing it.

4. Explain that "there are three things we do. . . ."

5. Buy another round because we're going to be talking for a while.

6. Say it's too complicated to explain well, but ask him/her the same question.

I see a bumper sticker on a car that reads VISUALIZE WORLD PEACE. I:

1. Try to imagine what peace must look like.

2. Imagine John Lennon's glasses.

3. Repeat those words to myself, kind of rolling them around: "World Peace."

4. Imagine what this tells me about the owner of the car.

5. Think: "Whirled peas."

6. Roll my eyes and murmur, "Damned Californians."

If I were an astronaut floating in space, the *first* thing I would do is:

1. Take a deep breath, relax, and take in the whole view.

2. Try to spot my house . . . or at least my continent.

3. Start describing what I saw.

4. Wish I had a camera.

5. Close my eyes.

6. Find a way to get back into the spacecraft.

Now add up your total score and divide it by 6. Here's how to rate yourself:

SCORE	CALCULATED PEN PREFERNCE
1–2.5	Black Pen (Hand me the pen!)
2.6–4.5	Yellow Pen (I can't draw, but . . .)
4.6–6	Red Pen (I'm not visual.)

There are two important takeaways from this exercise. The first is that depending on your visual thinking preference, you may find the greatest value in different sections in this book. If you're a Black Pen person and already feel confident about your ability to draw, I suspect that part II, which describes how to improve our ability to look and see, will be the most interesting place to start. If you're a Red Pen person and not convinced of the analytic power of pictures, you might want to start with part III (The Visual Thinking MBA) in order to see pictures at work in solving a business problem. If you're a Yellow Pen person, excellent at identifying what is most important, you might most appreciate part IV, as it describes how to show a picture to someone else.

The second takeaway from this exercise is even more powerful.

Regardless of visual thinking confidence or pen-color preference, everybody already has good visual thinking skills, and everybody can easily improve those skills.

Visual thinking is not a talent unique to select individuals, or limited only to people with years of dedicated study. Although your results on the pen-color assessment will help you find the best way to use this book, the most important thing to note is that regardless of how you scored, visual thinking is an ability in which we are all innately gifted. The proof is in the physiological, neurological, and biological systems we are born with and the sight-dependent intellectual, physical, and social abilities we learn from the beginning of our lives: namely, our amazing abilities to look, see, imagine, and show.

How to Use This Book

The essence of this book can be distilled down to one central idea.

Visual thinking is an extraordinarily powerful way to solve problems, and though it may appear to be something new, the fact is that we already know how to do it.

Although we are born with an amazing vision system, most of us rarely think about our visual abilities and even fewer have any idea how to improve them. It's as if we've been given a high-end desktop supercomputer as a gift, but we don't know where to find any new software. Even though sight is for most of us the most highly developed of all our senses, when it comes to visual thinking, we limit ourselves to what is available right out of the box. This is a shame, because by better understanding the vision tools that we already have (and then learning to use a few new ones) we can learn to solve problems with pictures in remarkable ways.

Think of this book as a guide rope that leads from here, where we have good but perhaps underutilized visual thinking skills, to there, where we have excellent visual thinking abilities that we can reliably call on whenever we need to. This guide rope is made up of three threads divided into strands, each a simple theme, each easy to explain, and easy to understand. These three threads are the process (*look, see, imagine, show*), our built-in biological tools (*eyes, mind's eye, hands/eyes*), and the ways we see (*who/what, how much, where, when, how, why*).

The Guide Rope to visual thinking

4 steps (process)

3 Parts (biology)

6 ways of seeing

1. **A four-step process: There is a learnable, repeatable, and useful process to visual thinking.**

   The backbone of this book is a very simple process. It is composed of just four steps, and the beauty of these steps is that we already know how to do all of them. In fact, we're so good at them that we don't consciously think about them at all. But by calling attention to these steps and drawing out the distinctions between them, we can instantly improve our understanding of how visual thinking works. In addition, by introducing tools and insights on this step-by-step basis, we can improve our abilities in a gradual and coordinated way.

2. **Three built-in tools to improve: In order to think visually, we rely on the interaction of our three "built-in" tools: our eyes, our mind's eye, and our hand-eye coordination. We can improve all three, and the better we get at one, the better we get at the others.**

   While our eyes serve as the tools by which we look at the world around us and see visual patterns within it, it is in our mind's eye where we manipulate those patterns, take them apart and rebuild them, hold them upside down and shake them in order to see what falls out. Then once we've rolled these patterns around and have something to explore, record, and share, we rely on coordination between our hands and our eyes to get those ideas down on paper for fine-tuning and sharing.

3. **Six ways of seeing: There are six fundamental questions that guide how we see things and then how we show things—and these six are recognizable to anyone.**

Regardless of business circumstance, project assignment, or timetable, every problem eventually breaks down into the six fundamental questions we've already seen. We're all familiar with these questions. Known as the 6 W's, they were introduced to us way back in elementary school as the basis of good storytelling: *who, what, when, where, how, why.* What makes the six exceptionally powerful for visual thinking is that these questions align precisely with the ways we literally see the world around us.

As we follow this guide rope through the book, these three themes are going to come up again and again. So, with pens in hand, we're ready to walk through the visual thinking process. But first, let's adjourn for a moment to the game room, where playing a hand of poker is going to help get things started.

CHAPTER 3

A GAMBLE WE CAN'T LOSE: THE FOUR STEPS OF VISUAL THINKING

Texas Hold 'em: The Table Stakes of Visual Thinking

One excellent way I've found to introduce people to visual thinking—especially to people who don't consider themselves visual—is to compare the process to playing a game of poker. In fact, I often begin visual thinking workshops by having everyone play a couple hands of Texas hold 'em. The game is simple enough that even people who have never played cards before can pick up the basics in a few minutes, and the lessons that the game teaches—how to look at a hand of cards and see patterns emerge, how to imagine what cards are necessary to complete the patterns, how to build the most effective hand to show other players—are textbook visual thinking.

Let me show you what I mean by walking quickly through a hand of hold 'em. Like any game of poker, the goal is to create the best combination of five cards, as shown in the following table.

In Texas hold 'em, each player receives two cards facedown that only he or she gets to look at. The dealer will turn another five cards faceup on the table for all players to see. From these seven cards (two "secret" and five "shared"), each player will construct his or her best possible hand.

Let's say, for example, that when you looked at your secret cards, you saw a jack and king of hearts.

Hand	Example				
Royal Flush	10♥	J♥	Q♥	K♥	A♥
Straight Flush	3♣	4♣	5♣	6♣	7♣
Four of a Kind	10♦	10♣	10♥	10♣	4♦
Full House	J♥	J♣	7♥	7♦	7♣
Flush	2♥	6♥	9♥	Q♥	K♥
Straight	3♥	4♣	5♦	6♣	7♥
Three of a Kind	9♣	9♦	9♥	6♣	2♠
Two Pairs	4♦	4♣	J♣	J♥	9♥
Pair	6♣	10♦	3♣	Q♦	10♣

Most Valuable
(least likely)

Least Valuable
(most likely)

Winning poker hands, most valuable to least valuable.

My cards

Because there are a lot of high-scoring combinations that could come your way, that's a great starting hand. So you place a good bet and the game keeps going. Step by step, the dealer then turns faceup the five shared cards on the table, and you see your hand getting better and better. You continue betting along the way since you imagine that the chances for someone else to have a better hand are becoming fewer and fewer.

As the dealer turns over the last shared card, you see that you've got a full house (a great hand in hold 'em), so you bet big. When those players still in the game show their cards, your full house is the winning hand, and you take the money.

Great. Now that you're feeling good about your poker skills, let's connect this game back to visual thinking. There are several reasons why the poker example works.

1. **There is a process, and rules to govern it.** Like any activity requiring a series of steps, poker has to be played in a specific order. The game wouldn't work if we first showed our entire hand, then placed our bets, and then dealt the cards. Similarly, visual thinking is also a process guided by rules.

2. **We must make decisions with less-than-perfect information.** In poker, we have to gamble at every step, guessing how things are going to play out long before we've seen all the cards. The same is true of visual thinking. We'll frequently have to make important decisions about which pictures to use before we have all the information.

3. **A complete visual language is made up of a small number of elements.** In poker, all the data is contained entirely within the fifty-two cards that make up the deck and the shared symbols on them. With nothing more that nine numbers (2, 3, 4, 5, 6, 7, 8, 9, 10), four faces (A, K, Q, J), four suits (hearts, diamonds, aces, spades), and two colors (red and black), there is still an infinite variety of ways to play the game. Likewise in visual thinking, a small set of visual cues will represent an infinite number of problem-solving options.

And the most important of all:

4. **The process of playing poker is a great analogy to the *process* of visual thinking.** First, we are handed a couple of cards and we *look* at them. Without looking at the cards, we have no ability to know what our chances of winning are, so without looking, there's no way for the game to begin.

   But just looking at the cards isn't enough to know what they tell us. Next we have to *see* what is on them. What color are they? What number or face do they contain? What suit are they? Do we have all the cards we should? Is anything missing? If *looking* is the semipassive process of collecting visual inputs, then *seeing* is the active process of selecting those visual inputs that matter most, and then recognizing the pattern-making components within them.

Once we've seen what we have in our hands, we next have to *imagine* how the emerging patterns might fit together. We have to imagine how the cards we've been dealt might create patterns that will help us win. We also need to imagine what the other players might have, and then try to imagine whether we can beat them or not.

The final step of the game is to *show*. At the end, everyone still playing has to lay their cards on the table and show what they've got. Unless someone at the table is an incredible bluffer with an inscrutable poker face and has fooled everyone else into folding early, nobody can win until everybody shows. The same is true of visual thinking. We may have imagined fantastic ideas, but unless we have a way to show them to others, the value of our ideas will never be known.

There we have it: **look, see, imagine, show.** The four steps of poker correspond exactly to the four steps of visual thinking. And as playing the game illustrates, there is nothing magic or secret about these steps. We complete these same steps in this same order every time we think visually.

The Process of Visual Thinking

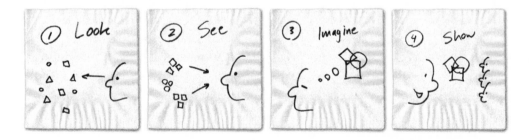

This process shouldn't come as a surprise. After all, we go through these steps thousands of times a day—like when we cross the street, for example. We look both ways and if we see a car nearby, we stop. If we see a car at a distance, we imagine whether we can make it across before it arrives, and if so, we show our decision by confidently striding across the street, or waiting until the car has safely passed by.

LOOK   SEE   IMAGINE   SHOW

The four-step visual thinking process when crossing a street.

Or when we prepare a business report: First we look at the materials we have to communicate; then we see what within them is most interesting, relevant, or useful; then we imagine the best way to convey our message; and then we show our report to our colleagues.

LOOK   SEE   IMAGINE   SHOW

The four-step visual thinking process when creating a report.

Or when we need to explain a chart in a business presentation: We look at what the chart contains (the key, the coordinates, the data sets, the sources), then we see what patterns emerge in the data (perhaps the x axis is rising faster than the y axis, or maybe the blue part of the pie chart is much larger than the red part), then we imagine what those patterns mean (costs are rising faster than profits; the Southwest region is outpacing the Northeast region), then we stand up and confidently show all these insights to our audience by walking them through exactly the same process we just completed ourselves.

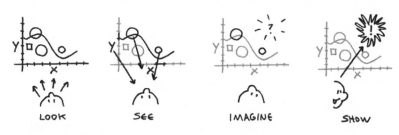

LOOK   SEE   IMAGINE   SHOW

The four-step visual thinking process when presenting a chart.

Because we're so good at this whole process, we don't think about it much. But that's only because we've practiced it so much that the process has become second nature. But watch a class of preschoolers holding hands on their way to the zoo, and we'll see that crossing the street safely isn't an intuitive process. Without the teachers as guides, many of the kids would walk right out into the street, in effect completing the *show* part of the process without having gone through the *look, see,* and *imagine* steps . . . with disastrous results. As we'll see later, that is exactly what most businesspeople do when creating a business graphic. And that's why it's worth spending a few more minutes learning the process.

THE VISUAL THINKING PROCESS, STEP BY STEP

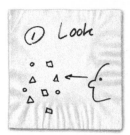

Looking

This is the semipassive process of taking in the visual information around us. Looking is about collecting inputs and making initial rough assessments of what's out there, so that we know how to respond. Looking involves scanning the environment in order to build an initial big-picture sense of things, while simultaneously asking the rapid-fire questions that help our minds make a first-pass assessment of what is in front of us.

> *Looking = Collecting and screening*

Looking *questions:*

- What is there? Is there a lot of it? What is not there?
- How far am I able to look? What are the edges and limits of my vision in this situation?
- What do I recognize right away, and what throws me off?
- Are the things in front of me what I expected to see? Can I "get" them rapidly, or do I need to spend extra time figuring out what I'm looking at?

Looking *activities:*

- Scan across the whole landscape. Build a big picture; note that there are forests and trees . . . and leaves, as well.
- Find the edges and determine which way is up. Establish the limits of our view and the fundamental coordinates of the data in front of us.
- Make an initial pass at screening out the noise; separate the visual wheat from the chaff.

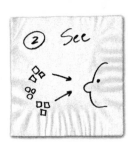

Seeing

This is the other side of the visual *input* coin, and it is where our eyes get more consciously active. While we were just looking, we were scanning the whole scene and collecting initial inputs. Now that we're seeing, we are selecting which inputs are worth more detailed inspection. This is based on recognizing patterns—sometimes consciously, oftentimes not.

> **Seeing = Selecting and clumping**

Seeing *questions:*

- Do I know what I'm seeing? Have I seen this before?
- Are any patterns emerging? Does anything in particular stand out?

- What can I take away from what I see—what patterns, what priorities, what interactions—to help me make enough sense of this environment in order to make decisions about it?

- Do I have enough visual inputs collected to make sense of what I see, or do I need to go back and keep looking?

Seeing *activities:*

- Filter for relevance: Actively select those visual inputs worth another look and dismiss others. (Then later go back and check again.)

- Categorize and make distinctions: Separate the wheat into different categories by type.

- Notice patterns and clump creatively; identify visual commonalities among inputs, and larger commonalities among categories.

Imagining

Imagining is what happens after the visuals have been collected and selected, and the time comes to start manipulating them. Imagining can best be thought of in one of two ways: It is either the act of seeing with our eyes closed or the act of seeing something that isn't there.

> **Imagining = Seeing what isn't there**

Imagining *questions:*

- Where have I seen this before? Can I make any analogies to things I've seen in the past?

- Are there better ways to configure the patterns I see? Can I rearrange them to make more sense?

- Can I manipulate the patterns so that something invisible becomes visible?

- Is there a hidden framework connecting everything I saw? Can I use that framework as a place to put other things that I've seen?

Imagining activities:

- Close your eyes to see more: With all visual inputs fresh in the mind, look with your eyes closed and see if new connections emerge.

- Find analogies: Ask, "Where have I seen this before?" and then imagine how analogous solutions might work in this new situation.

- Manipulate the patterns: Turn pictures upside down, flop them left to right, switch coordinates to turn them inside out. See if something new becomes visible.

- Alter the obvious: Push visual ideas by finding multiple ways to show the same thing.

Showing

Once we've found patterns, made sense of them, and figured out a way to manipulate them to discover something new, we've got to show it all to others. We need to summarize all that we've seen, find the best framework for visually representing our ideas, nail things down on paper, point out what we imagined, and then answer our audience's questions.

> **Showing = Making it all clear**

Showing questions:

- Of all I've imagined, what are the three most important pictures that emerged—both for me and for my audience?

- What is the best way to visually convey my idea? Which visual framework will be most appropriate for sharing what I've seen?

- When I go back to what I originally looked at, does what I'm now showing still make sense?

- Say, "This is what I saw." Then ask your audience, "Does it make sense to you? Do you see the same things, or do you see something different?"

Showing *activities:*

- Clarify your best ideas: Prioritize all visual ideas so that the most relevant come to the top.

- Nail things down: Pick the appropriate visual framework and get your ideas down on paper or up on the board.

- Cover all the W's: Make sure that *who/what, how much, where,* and *when* are always visible; let *how* and *why* emerge as the visual punch line.

It's Not Always Linear, Actually

For the rest of this book, these are the four steps that we're going to take every time we solve a problem with a picture. In fact, the rest of this book is built around these steps. But there's one more nuance to be aware of that will help us as we apply the process. Looking back to poker, we can see one place in particular where the game diverges from visual thinking: namely, forgiveness. In poker, rules are rules, and once you've laid your money down, you can never go back. But when solving problems with pictures, going back and making changes is one of the most valuable parts of the whole approach.

Here's a useful process secret. Although the four steps will always naturally flow in order, we don't have to march through them in a straight 1-2-3-4 line. In fact, the whole process plays out more like a series of loops, something like the drawing at the right.

Notice how looking and seeing go

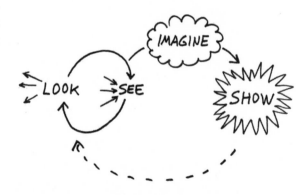

The visual thinking process, as it really happens.

around and around, feeding off each other? These two steps that bring in visual information are so closely linked that one simply can't happen without the other. But that doesn't mean we can't take advantage of their differences as we improve our visual thinking skills—on the contrary, in the next two chapters we're going to see how this loop actually helps us.

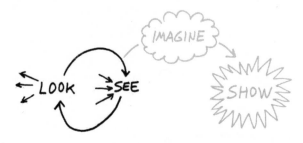

In a very different way, imagining—taking everything that we've collected and selected and then seeing it all with our eyes closed—is the bridge that leads us from having visual information *come in* to helping us get our visuals *out*. We're going to talk a lot about this almost magical step, and provide a new tool to help make imagining a more reliable and less mysterious activity.

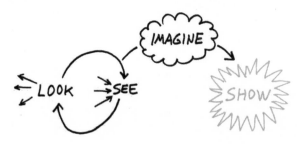

Last comment on the process: Did you see that big dotted-line arrow connecting *show* back to *look/see*? The point is this: If we've done our job right, the moment we start to show our work to other people, they will start their own visual thinking process, look-ing at our pictures, seeing what is interesting to them, and imagining how they could manipulate and alter what we're showing. So the visual thinking loop continues again and again.

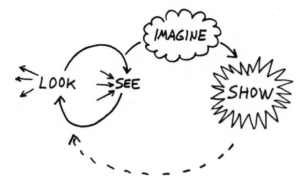

PART II
DISCOVERING IDEAS

Looking Better, Seeing Sharper, Imagining Further:
Tools and Rules for Good Visual Thinking

CHAPTER 4

NO THANKS, JUST LOOKING

One reason that most people are uncertain about how to approach problem solving with pictures is that most people are unsure of their ability to draw. Red Pen and Yellow Pen people in particular may believe that since they *can't draw*, they can't rely on visual thinking as a way to approach complex challenges. It's unfortunate, because this belief stops many of the most potentially insightful visual thinkers from ever getting started.

Let's turn this thinking around. Instead of believing that we first need to be able to draw (*show*), let's imagine for the moment that being able to draw well is largely an outcome of being able to *see* well, and being able to see well comes directly from being able to *look* well. In other words:

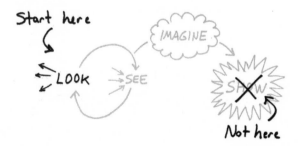

Understanding visual thinking as a complete process means that the starting point isn't learning to draw better, it's learning to look better. That's why the process is valuable: It puts looking—something we're all innately good at—back at the front of the line.

Viewed from this perspective, the best way to start thinking visually is to become better acquainted with how our internal vision system looks at the world.

How We Look

Every second that our eyes are open, millions of visual signals enter as photons of light, are converted into electrical impulses by our retinas, and then get passed along our optic nerves into various regions of our brains where the signals are parsed, filtered, compared, categorized, and recombined—so that they emerge as the complete pictures that we *see* inside our heads.

This entire process takes place hundreds of times every second, completely unconsciously, and neuroscientists and vision specialists are only now beginning to comprehend how it all works. The more they learn, the more fantastic and almost magical the mechanisms of vision appear. Yet as amazing as our automatic looking system is, it is only part of the looking involved in visual thinking. When we talk about visual thinking, we're talking about hijacking this automatic system in order to consciously take advantage of its strengths. When we talk about visual thinking, we're first talking about *active looking*.

Which Way Is Up?

Although the basic neurological pathways of vision* remain the same whether we're looking at the stars in a night sky, a child's face, or a spreadsheet of numbers, *what* our eyes look at and *how* we make sense of it depends on the visual problem that we're trying to solve at any given time.

Imagine that we're going to meet some friends for bowling. What's the first thing that we look at when we walk into the bowling alley? The placement of the number-six pin in the twelfth lane? The numbers printed on the back of the bowling shoes behind the desk? No, the first problem that we face is simply understanding where we are, so our eyes scan the width of the whole bowling alley, establishing the limits of the space and in a split-second creating a three-dimensional mental model of which way is up, where the walls are, and where we are located. Before we've even had a chance to think about it, our automatic looking process

How we look depends on the problem we need to solve.

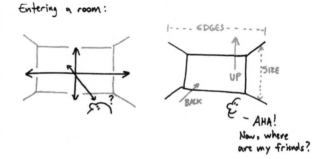

When we first enter an environment, our eyes make a quick three-dimensional model to establish the space's orientation and our position within it.

---

* If you're interested in the scientific rationale for much of what I'm about to say, see Appendix A: The Science of Visual Thinking.

has already established that the bowling alley is this wide, that deep, so tall, and—thankfully—not upside down. In other words, our visual autopilot has established our orientation and position.

With this 3-D bowling alley model in our heads, our looking system gets to work on the job at hand, namely finding our friends. Our eyes automatically scan for telltale signs: a familiar face, a distinctive profile, a telling movement, etc. Bingo! There they are: three lanes over, just past the soda machine. Through unconscious *identification* and *recognition*—matching what we're looking at with what we've expected to see—we've found our friends.

When we've got a rough idea of *where* we are, we start looking for people or things that we recognize (that match our expectations of *who* or *what* should be there).

Only later—once we've got our bowling shoes on, have our ball in hand, and are standing at the top of the lane—are our eyes really interested in looking in the precise *direction* of the pins down at the far end.

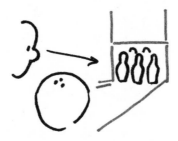

Only when we're finally ready to roll the ball do we really look in the precise direction of the pins.

It's worth emphasizing these *orientation, position, identification,* and *direction* steps because they are just four of the key tasks that our looking system automatically takes care of for us. These four are particularly important because if they are not completed instantly—if we have to spend a lot of time and effort figuring out which way is up—we will never have the chance to move on with rolling our strike.

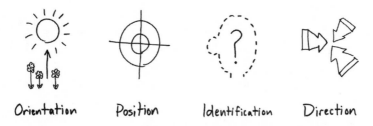

Orientation   Position   Identification   Direction

Four of the automatic looking tasks—things our vision system takes care of without any conscious thought from us—include orientation, position, identification, and direction.

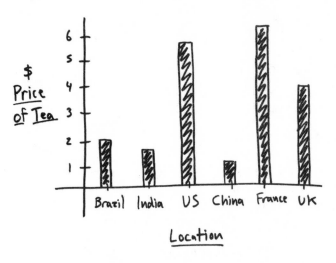

Let's start with this basic business chart.

What's important here is that these same four looking tasks define whether we immediately "get" a business picture or not. To illustrate what I mean, let's start with a basic visual thinking task, like reviewing a simple chart.

With just a couple seconds' review, it should be obvious that this chart compares the price of tea across a set of countries. But what makes that obvious? What is it about this chart that allows us to understand quickly what it shows? Using what we've learned about looking, let's find out.

First off, the chart follows a set of generally accepted standards on how we present data with a picture: It is based on a horizontal and vertical two-axis coordinate system.

Just like the ceiling, walls, and floor that our eyes noted the instant that we entered the bowling alley, this chart gives us the visual cues to immediately understand which way is up. In this chart, these cues come in the form of the two-axis coordinate system indicated by the main vertical and horizontal lines. Of course, up isn't really "up" at all (here, it's *how much*), and right isn't really "right" (it's *where*), but our eyes still recognize the simple coordinate system.

Are there any other ways this chart is "obvious"? Yes. The labels allow us to find our *position* relative to the coordinates and to the other countries. If we're in the United States, for example, we can find ourselves near the center of the chart.

Finally, the relative positions of the countries and prices and the various heights of the price measurement bars all work to give us a sense of *direction,* in this case, where countries' teas prices are relative to one another. For example, we see that tea is much more expensive in the United States than in China, but slightly less than in France.

The point here is to illustrate that even though this chart and the bowling alley have nothing in common, our eyes still *look* at them the same way. We have exactly the same number of incoming visual signals, the same kind of electrical impulses to analyze and collate, and the same pathways along which to pass those impulses. From our eyes' perspective, we've even got the same set of problems to solve—*orientation, position, identification,* and *direction.*

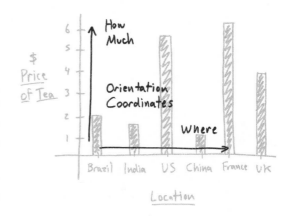

The chart allows us to quickly establish orientation by providing us with a horizontal and vertical coordinate system.

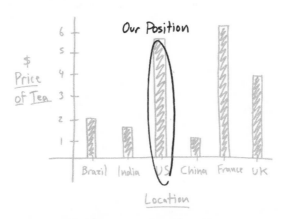

By providing labels, the chart allows us to determine our own position relative to the coordinates and to the other listed countries.

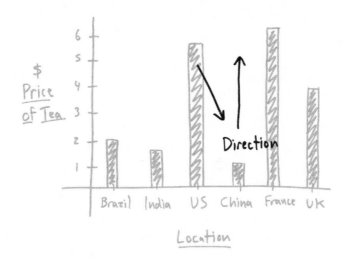

The relative heights of the vertical bars tell us the direction—up, down, the same, etc.—of one price to another.

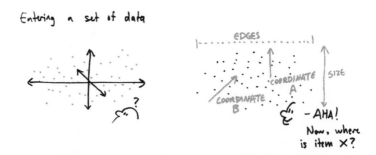

When we enter any "data landscape" (a spreadsheet, table, chart, diagram, etc.), our eyes go through the same looking process as when we entered the bowling alley.

How to Look Better: Four Rules to Live By

To develop good looking skills—and build a good foundation for visual thinking—there are four basic rules to apply every time we look at something new:

1. Collect everything we can to look at—the more the better (at least at first).

2. Have a place where we can lay out everything and really look at it all, side by side.

3. Always define a basic coordinate system to give us clear orientation and position.

4. Find ways to cut ruthlessly from everything our eyes bring in—we need to practice *visual triage.*

THE FOUR CARDINAL RULES FOR BETTER LOOKING

① Collect everything you can.

> **Looking Rule 1: Collect everything possible up front.**

Looking is collecting, just like any other kind of collecting. Once we've started, we're immediately faced with one of two problems—either having too much to collect or not enough. The first situation we've already seen in chapter 2: When Daphne needed to make a decision about her publishing company's brand, she collected all kinds of data about the industry, so much, in fact, that she couldn't quickly make sense of the results.

These days, Daphne's problem is shared by everyone, everywhere, in every business context: Information overload is today's standard operating condition, and we're just going to have to learn to deal with it. Given that reality, *active* looking serves as a useful approach for figuring out what's important and making sense of it. After all, our eyes have too much information coming in all the time, and yet we can still see very well. There's a lesson there.

Too Much to Look At

When Daphne e-mailed all her survey materials to our team, it was as if we were suddenly teleported into the middle of the bowling alley, bypassing the front door and finding ourselves plopped down in the middle of a lane, with data sailing past us right and left. Without knowing where we'd come in—or even what we were supposed to be looking for—we didn't know where to look first.

But our vision system is flexible and resilient, and it really wants to figure things out. So we put our active looking process to work. First order of business? Figure out which way is up. We needed to find a coordinate system to get us pointed upright, so we defined a model that mapped *who/what (competitors)* versus *how much (revenue)*.

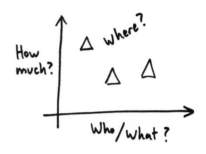

Next up: *position*. We looked for measures that showed *where* Daphne's company sat in the space defined by our coordinate system. Next: *identification*. We looked through the data to locate where other companies were located within the same space. Eventually, the picture that became Daphne's chart emerged. Information overload is here to stay, but active looking gives us a way to get through the worst of it.

Choosing a who/what versus a how much coordinate system gave us a context in which to look at other detailed data, such as where and when.

Not Enough to Look At

A year after completing Daphne's publishing brand strategy picture, I was contacted by Ken, the communications director at a well-known scientific research center, with what appeared to be a problem similar to Daphne's, namely how to position his institution's "name brand" for maximum financial impact. The scientific institution that Ken worked for also needed to raise awareness among potential investors—not because it was going to list on the stock exchange, but because changes in the federal funding landscape prompted it to look into possible alternative sources of scientific funding outside of the federal government.

But it quickly became clear that Ken's challenge was actually the precise opposite of Daphne's: She had too much to look at; he did not have enough. It came down to the ways the two organizations looked at themselves. Daphne's company saw itself as a money-making business, and any opportunity to make more money was at least worth a look. Ken's institution saw itself as a guardian of scientific truth, and was uncomfortable with potential conflicts of interest from business sources of funding—so uncomfortable that our entire study had to take place under the cover of darkness. If word got out internally that we were even *looking* at funding options, scientific mutiny was feared.

We were again thrown into the bowling alley, but this time with most of the lights switched off. We had the institution's insights and reports on federal funding, but that lit up only so much. If the institution was going to look outside for money, it was going to need to look outside for ideas. As with Daphne's challenge, we had to define our coordinates first. Again, we started with the 6 W's as a way to frame the problem:

- *Who:* Who were roughly similar organizations—science based, academic and research oriented, focused on the natural world—and in need of large sums of nongovernmental money?

- *How much:* How much money did these organizations need, and how much did they get?

- *Where:* Where does their money come from? Where are they located in the overall landscape of scientific and natural sciences funding?

- *When:* How often do they get their money? Weekly? Annually? All the time?

With these framing criteria in place, we went out and looked for the right *whos*. We found numerous organizations worth including—museums, environmental organizations . . . everything from Conservation International to the Sierra Club to the Monterey Bay Aquarium—they all fit in the frame: *science, natural world, needs money*. So we took names, and between the laws of public disclosure and the miracle of the Internet, we were quickly able to find much of what we were looking for: size of organization, financial status, source of funds, etc.

With nothing to start with other than a simple problem statement—"What are nongovernmental ways we can get funding?"—we used active looking to collect the pieces necessary to build a visual model of the natural sciences funding landscape. It looked roughly like this.

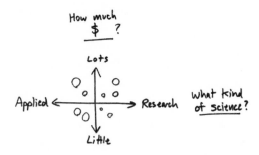

Visual model of the natural sciences funding landscape.

With that framework in place, it was now a matter of plotting in the numbers we'd collected, and we were on our way toward looking at the viability of all kinds of funding options. Once again, active looking provided the guidance we needed, even in darkness.

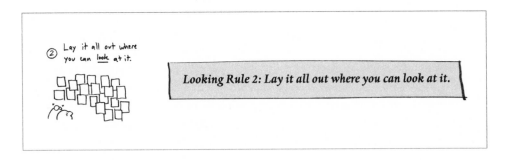

Having collected everything, we now have to lay it all out where we can really look at it. This is such an obvious rule that it often gets ignored, and yet it is the single best way to effectively look at a broad range of inputs—take everything we've collected and lay it out side by side, where our eyes can scan it all in a few passes.

The Garage-Sale Principle:
How Do We Even Know What We've Got?

Let's call this the garage-sale principle: Regardless of how well organized all the stuff in our garage may be, laying everything out on tables in the light of day yields a completely new perspective on it all. The same is true of data: When it is packed away in individual files and records, it's impossible to look at the big picture—but getting everything out in the open makes otherwise invisible connections visible.

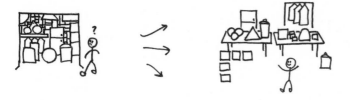

The garage-sale principle: Everything looks different when we can see it all at once.

A couple years ago, I was working with a computer manufacturer in Silicon Valley. In order to keep up with global changes in software sales, the CEO of this company made the gutsy decision to turn his sales process upside down. No longer would customers buy a shrink-wrapped package of software CDs and then receive complimentary upgrades and technical support. In the new world that the CEO envisioned, the software itself would be given away for free, and customers would pay for the upgrades and support—kind of like going from a "buy a book a month" club to joining an expensive private library: The same books are available; we just pay for them differently.

This was a huge change. It meant that *everything* had to be revised, from the way software was written to the support process. In order to avoid company-wide panic among the tens of thousands of employees, the decision was made that the first word should go out through a series of low-key, "impromptu" meetings—hundreds of them.

What a disaster. From the moment that the designated speaker first mentioned the change, he was overwhelmed. Salespeople demanded, "What about commissions?" Engineers demanded, "How will we release the binaries?" Everybody demanded, "Are we insane?!"

All the speaker could say was, "Let me finish. I promise we'll get to that! For now I just want us to look at the big picture!"

The problem was that there was no picture at all. It was as if he had said that everything in the garage was going to be rearranged, but nobody could look in the garage—all they could look at was their own little stack of boxes. It's too bad, because the message to deliver was simple and almost entirely visual—*here's what we do now, here's what it will look like in the future, here are the parts that will be the most difficult to change*—and could easily have been introduced with no more than two or three pictures.

But no pictures were ever made. These meetings went on for weeks, with the same result every time: shock followed by confusion followed by anxiety. In the end, momentum finally built up enough to where people either got on board or left the company. Today the company is well along the path to implementing the change, fine-tuning the new process, and waiting to see how the market reacts. But when I think about the time and money that was wasted in those meetings and the angst they generated, all I can think is how much could have been saved by simply laying out the big issues side by side on the table and letting everybody just take a look.

WHERE CAN WE PUT EVERYTHING SO THAT WE CAN LOOK AT IT?

From a practical perspective, laying everything out where we can look at it means we need plenty of space, so it's important to be prepared to spread things out and let the room get messy. Cover every table, chair, wall, and flat space: It's amazing the connections that our eyes will find when given free reign to look everywhere.

When I was still working for the company that sent me to London, my team had to present a design to a client. The day before the presentation, I asked everyone to print out a copy of everything they had created, from notebook sketches to typeface tests to final designs, and pile them all in a stack in the conference room. When I came in early the next morning to set up the room, the table overflowed. When Susi, the receptionist, arrived thirty minutes later, the conference room looked like a war zone, with papers spread from end to end.

Susi freaked. Our boss Roger was notorious for neatness—especially in the conference room. Here I was, ankle deep in paper and, even worse, taping things to the walls. When she saw that, Susi really went buggy. The only thing I could do was ask for her help.

It was a great day. When our clients arrived, a surprising thing happened. We couldn't start the meeting. As people moved into the room, they immediately gravitated toward the walls; fingers pointed, arms waved, designers and clients who had never spoken before spontaneously conversed—and great ideas emerged as people really looked at everything for the first time.

At some point during the presentation, I noticed that Roger was in the room. He smiled, and after the meeting he insisted that the work remain on the walls for several days, to let other people coming and going in the office take a look. In the end, the final design emerged not from a formal review, but from the perceptive comments of an accountant who couldn't stop looking at two of the drawings.

But big open spaces aren't always needed to lay everything out. Many times the data we need to look at is just that: numbers, plain and simple. That's where spreadsheets come in. Although some Black Pen people may be convinced that numbers buried in rows and columns can never be "visual," spreadsheets are excellent tools for *spreading* out lots of data on a single *sheet,* where it can all be looked at and compared in one go.

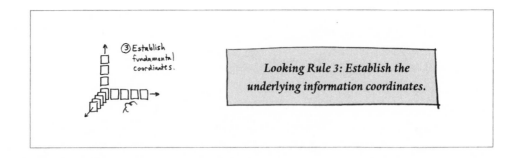

③ Establish fundamental coordinates.

Looking Rule 3: Establish the underlying information coordinates.

Remember that instant 3-D model of the bowling alley that we created in our minds the moment we walked in? We were able to build it so quickly because our eyes could immediately discern the room's underlying coordinate system: which way was up, left, right, front, back. Since we live in a three-dimensional world, our eyes are really good at recognizing these coordinates, otherwise known as length, height, and depth. As an example, imagine holding a small box.

To represent the three-dimensional space that the box occupies, we can draw a three-dimensional grid around it, where the coordinates are called *x* (length), *y* (height), and *z* (depth).

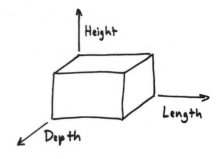

A box has three dimensions: length, height, and depth.

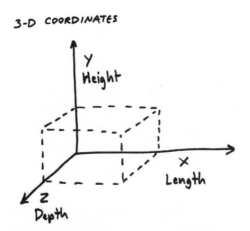

3-D COORDINATES

When we represent the box in a coordinate system, we label the axes *x*, *y*, and *z*.

Now imagine that the box is a room that we're inside. Even though it looks a little different because we're inside it, the underlying coordinates are the same, and we're still looking at length, height, and depth.

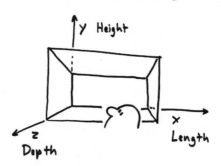

SEEN FROM THE INSIDE:

Any room that we're inside can be drawn
on these same x, y, z coordinates.

Red Pen people might find this idea confusing, but no worries, our vision system does not. After all, this is exactly what our system is doing a hundred times per second—looking for visual cues to help determine the x, y, and z of the world around us.

Fine, but How Can We Look at an Idea?

But what happens when we're looking at things that don't exist in three dimensions, things such as the price of tea in China, Daphne's industry data, or Ken's funding information? How can coordinates help us find the underlying shape of an *idea*?

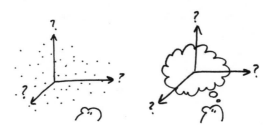

How can we find coordinates that frame raw data, information, and ideas?

The trick is to find a coordinate system that doesn't rely on length, height, or depth, and guess what? We've already got one, six, in fact.

We've encountered this new coordinate system several times already in this book: the 6 W's. Perhaps we've never thought of *who/what, how much, when, where, how,* and *why*

WHO/WHAT, HOW MUCH, WHERE, WHEN, HOW, WHY

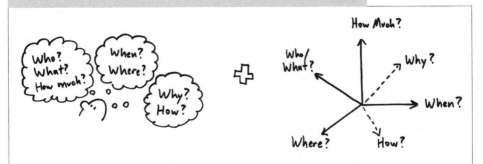

The 6 W's aren't just a set of questions we ask to define a problem. They're also the source of every pictorial coordinate system we're going to use from now on.

as a coordinate system, but that's exactly the way we're going to use them for the rest of this book.

Here's how it works: Think back to the picture we drew for Daphne. It was a chart that compared *who* to *how much* to *where*. Think back to Ken's picture: It was a chart that compared *what* to *how much*, then plotted in *who*.

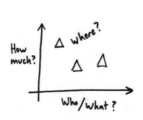

Daphne's picture: *who* versus *how much* versus *where*.

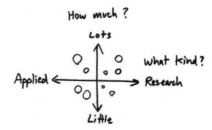

Ken's picture: *what* versus *how much*.

A stock price chart compares *how much* to *when*. A table of the winning times in a race compares *who* to *when*. Even a world map is really just a *where* (N-S) superimposed on another *where* (W-E), with some *what* (continents) placed on top.

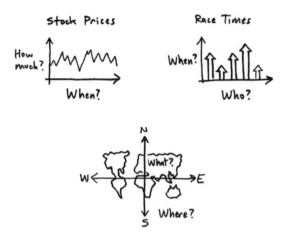

The 6 W's are used as coordinates for almost every descriptive picture we're likely to face.

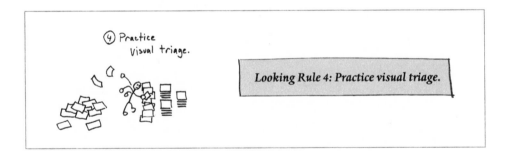

Looking Rule 4: Practice visual triage.

Think about any movie or television show you've watched that includes scenes of an emergency room: *M*A*S*H*, *ER*, *Pearl Harbor*, *Band of Brothers*. Now think about the scene where the big crash / accident / battle has just taken place, and the wounded are piling up faster than the doctors can help them. What happens every time? A senior nurse runs out into the chaos and starts making instant, intuition-and-experience-based decisions about who has enough chance of survival to be admitted, and who must be left out in the cold. This is called "triage," and our eyes do it all the time.

Here's why: There is always far more visual information out there than we can process, so our vision system needs to be picky about what it lets past the front door. Although most of this process remains a mystery, our brain's higher processing centers benefit from the end result. It is as if our eyes have some kind of experiential intuition—just like the triage nurse who has seen it all—that helps them make instant judgment calls about what is important to look at and what is not.

What Do We Look at First?

This "intuition" is actually the result of many "low-level" cognitive processes. These are the activities that take place when we first receive sensory inputs and react to them without putting demands on our brain's more complex capabilities. When we look up to watch a plane fly by and instead squeeze our eyes closed to avoid the sun, we're experiencing a "low-level" mental process—in this case a simple instinctive reaction. Because we act before we even think about it, such actions are called "precognitive responses" and the sensory inputs that cause them—in this case the bright intensity of the sun—are called "precognitive attributes."

As visual signals enter our eyes, our visual processing centers take a quick glance at everything, make a rapid decision about what's really worth looking at, then pass that signal on down the line, rejecting everything else. This visual triage works because visual precognitive attributes are everywhere, and our eyes know exactly how to recognize them, without even thinking about it.

PRECOGNITIVE VISUAL TRIAGE

Neuroscientists and psychologists have discovered evolutionary reasons why we're so well adapted to rapidly recognizing and processing many precognitive attributes. We're good at distinguishing vertical from horizontal lines because they help us keep upright in a vertical and horizontal world; we're good at interpreting shading and shadows because they indicate where the sun is, telling us which way is up; we're good at picking up subtle differences in visual textures because they help us find the edges of objects, etc.

Precognitive visuals are those that we process long before we even know that we are processing them.

Knowing about these precognitive cues is useful because it helps us identify which kinds of pictures (or pieces of pictures) we're going to understand without any conscious mental effort. If the goal of our visual triage nurse is to let in only those visual signals that provide the greatest meaning but have the lowest impact, she is going to look kindly at these kinds of visual signals and let them come right in.

The point here is that the more precognitive cues there are in a picture, the more likely we are to move the picture to the front of the line and process it quickly, saving our "high-level" mental capacity for deeper analytic processing: the kind that we'll see in the next chapter.

Proximity: Our eyes assume that things closer to each other are related.

Proximity   •• •• •• ••

Color: Our eyes immediately notice differences in color and assume groupings based on like coloring.

Color   • • • ○ • • • •

Size: Our eyes perceive differences in size with essentially zero effort, again allowing the assumption that the odd one is the one worth noting.

Size   • • • • • ● • •

Orientation: Our eyes instantly distinguish between vertical and horizontal orientation (but have a much harder time with angles other than 90 degrees).

Orientation   – – – – – | – –

Direction: "Fate" is another word for perceived movement, something that we also pick up on without any conscious thought (and which will become key in the next chapter).

"Fate"
(Direction)

Shape: Our eyes notice differences in shapes somewhat less well.

Shape   • ■ ▲ ▮ ▬ ◆ ▲ ▮

Shading: But our eyes immediately detect differences in shading as a way of distinguishing between up and down or in and out.

Shading   ◔ ◕ ⬤ ◑ ◔ ◕

Common precognitive visual attributes: visual cues that help us rapidly determine what is worth looking at and what is not.

CHAPTER 5

THE SIX WAYS OF SEEING

While *looking* is about collecting the raw visual information that is in front of us, *seeing* is about selecting what's important. Here's the difference: Imagine that you're driving along and suddenly your car's engine gives a heave and starts hammering. You pull over and turn off the key. The engine dies with a shudder and a puff of blue smoke. You climb out, pop the hood, and lean in. Your eyes begin roving over the engine compartment from front to back, and side to side, taking it all in: hoses, headers, manifolds, cables, wires, filters, dipsticks, fan belts. There's a lot of stuff in there, some of which you may recognize, some a total mystery. You know something is wrong, but you don't know what. So your eyes just roam. *That's looking.*

Then your eyes catch on something over to the left, where a group of thick wires emerge from a black plastic cap, like spaghetti from a pasta maker. All the wires flow out and attach to the side of the engine . . . except one. That particular wire isn't going any-where—unlike the others, it's just hanging there. Your eyes pick up on this broken pattern, and although you might not know anything about engines, you do know that it just doesn't seem right. Then you notice a place on the engine where it appears that it should attach, just like the others. Hmmm . . . perhaps attaching the noodle there would fix the problem? *That's seeing.*

Looking at
a problem

Seeing a
problem

Looking at a problem is how we start, but *just looking* doesn't present any solutions. In order to know what to fix, we need to be able to *see* what's broken.

The differences between these two go beyond semantics. Our eyes do very different things when we look and when we see, and both are necessary for visual problem solving. Depending on our level of familiarity with auto mechanics, we may have known exactly what we were looking at when we popped the hood, or have been completely lost. But even if we were lost, there was still a very good chance that our eyes might pick up on something wildly out of place. That kind of contextual pattern recognition is what seeing is about, and our eyes do it extraordinarily well.

Seeing is the flip side of looking: Looking is the open process of collecting visual information, seeing is the narrowing process of putting the visual pieces together in order to make sense of them. Looking is collecting; seeing is selecting and identifying patterns. And really good seeing is even more than just pattern recognition; good seeing is problem recognition.

One of the reasons that pictures are such a great way to solve problems is that many problems are hard to see clearly, and a picture can help us see aspects of the problem that might otherwise be invisible. Visual thinking helps by giving us a way to see problems not as an endless variety of things that go wrong, but as a small set of interconnected visual challenges, each one of which can be pictured more clearly on its own.

Seeing the Whole Picture

Over the following several pages, we're going to complete a visualization drill that will show us something new about how we see. In this exercise we're going to conjure up a series of simple mental images, mentally animate them, and then watch them come to life—all in our mind's eye. In order for this to work, it will be helpful for you to sit in a quiet place where it's possible to read a few lines and then look away from this book for a moment while you mentally conjure up what you've just read.

I call this the bird-dog drill, and when it is complete, you will see that we don't see in just one way at all. Depending on the problem in front of us, we can see in several different ways: up to six different ways, in fact . . . which just happen to map exactly back to those same 6 W's.

So find a quiet spot for the next ten minutes, and let's do the bird-dog drill.

THE BIRD-DOG DRILL

1. Picture someone you know who makes you feel good.

We're going to start with something easy to visualize, namely a person, someone familiar to you. In your mind's eye, I want you to picture someone who you know personally, someone who just the thought of makes you feel good. If you're a parent, it might be your child; if you're married, perhaps your spouse; if you're unmarried, your boy- or girlfriend; if you don't have a boy- or girlfriend, perhaps your best friend.

It doesn't matter who it is, but it does matter that thinking about them makes you feel happy.

Once you've come up with who the person is, I'd like you to picture them in your mind's eye, even in just a general way. Don't worry about seeing every detail of their face, don't worry too much about what they're wearing—just say their name to yourself and see what image comes to you.

2. Picture your favorite dog.

While keeping that image filed away at the top of your mind for quick retrieval, I want you to think about your favorite dog. Be specific: Think about the first dog you ever had, or the one you have now. If you've never had a dog, that's OK, just think of Lassie. In any case, see again if you can create a general image in your mind that shows "dog."

3. Picture someone pushing a baby carriage.

A few more characters to go: Next, I want you to picture a couple pushing a baby carriage. In this case, we don't need any details of the people or the baby carriage, just a rough image of what two people pushing a baby carriage look like. Now, file that one away for a moment while we create our last character.

4. Picture a bird.

Last character: I want you to think of a bird. A seagull, an eagle, a crow, a robin, a pelican . . . just name a bird and think for a moment about what it looks like. Got it? Good.

OK, we've got our cast of characters.

- Someone who makes you feel good
- Your favorite dog
- A couple pushing a baby carriage
- A bird

5. Picture an outdoor place where there is a bench you can sit on. Sit on it.

It's time to make a little scene. Picture a place in your favorite park, someplace where there is a bench you can sit on where you can relax and just watch the people passing by. I often think of the Marina Green in San Francisco: a sandy path along the grassy edge of the Bay, water behind framed by the Golden Gate Bridge, a paradise-on-earth kind of place. Find your own place and, in your mind's eye, put yourself on that bench.

6. See your full scene.

Now we're going to populate this scene with your cast of characters. First off, just a little way in front of you is your friend, walking the dog on a leash. Coming from the other direction toward your friend and your dog is the baby carriage couple. Somewhere a little ways away, beyond the baby carriage, the bird is sitting on the grass.

Let the scene play along for a moment. Perhaps your friend pets the dog, perhaps the dog sniffs in the dirt, perhaps the couple with the baby carriage slowly moves along this way, perhaps the bird is pecking at the ground—lots of little things are taking place as the scene comes alive.

Then . . . uh-oh, what's this? The dog spots the bird. The dog stops, looks, sniffs the air. Now what? Does the dog move toward the bird? Does your friend see the bird? Does the carriage keep rolling? Does the dog dart forward? Does the leash pull tight? Watch for a moment and see what plays out. Let it go for a few seconds. . . .

Stop the scene right here. Game over: Freeze things in your mind as much as you can and try to lock down what's what and where's where. We're going to talk about what you just saw, but before we do, one question: Is the bird still on the ground, or did it fly away?

The Six Ways We See

As you think about answering the question, let's take a look at what just happened. By creating this scene based on a few simple images, we built a scale model of how we see.

Granted, it was completely artificial and consciously forced, but the basic mental methodology and mechanisms of seeing all took place.

As we went through that drill, whether our eyes were closed or open, whether it was easy to complete or a real struggle, we did *see* a lot. A bunch of events took place throughout our vision system, many simultaneously, some just split seconds apart, some over the entire duration of the exercise. Broadly speaking, what follows are the six ways we see.

1. WE SAW OBJECTS—THE WHO AND THE WHAT

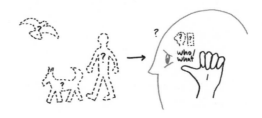

One of the first things that happened as we created this scene was that we saw several *objects:* There was our friend, there was a dog, there was a bird, there was a bench. They are all objects we know, that have names, and that are visually distinct. I doubt that anyone had a hard time visually distinguishing the dog from the baby carriage, for example.

There could also have been a whole lot of other objects that our minds also placed in the scene, whether we intentionally conjured them up or not—perhaps some trees, water, grass, clouds, other people and dogs—most anything that we'd expect to see in such a scene is possible.

The way that we created and recognized these objects was by seeing their measurable aspects and their qualitative attributes. Whether we were aware of it or not, we knew our friend through recalling countless measurements of facial feature size, proportion, and placement: Our mind's eye created a visual shorthand version of our friend's face based on countless such measurements stored away in our brain's neocortex.* The dog showed similar visual specifics depending on the breed we chose: size, color, hair length, etc., all of which we saw to a greater or lesser degree in our mind's eye. The baby carriage was round or square in shape, pink or orange or blue in color; the bird was white, black, blue, long neck, short neck—the list is endless. The point is that we recognized *who* and *what* we were seeing because we saw them as discrete objects exhibiting known measures and attributes.

2. WE SAW QUANTITIES—THE *HOW MANY AND HOW MUCH*

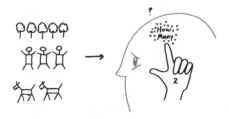

While part of our mind was occupied with visually identifying objects, another part was seeing numbers. We saw one dog, one bird, and at least three people. The baby carriage had four wheels (or maybe three, if it was one of those sporty tricycle jobs seen in places like the San Francisco marina). The bird had two wings, the dog had four legs, and who knows how many trees there might have been. If we saw ourselves in a park, probably too many to even attempt counting.

Recognizing these *how manys* and *how muchs* was also near instantaneous, and again, we didn't confuse the number of objects with the objects themselves. We didn't mix up "four" and "legs on the dog," for example. The point here is that our minds didn't have any trouble simultaneously seeing things as well as quantities of those things, and we didn't have to get hung up on the individual qualitative details of the objects in order

---

* If you're interested in the neurobiology and science behind the six ways we see, be sure to read Appendix A: The Science of Visual Thinking.

to see how many of each there were. So far then, we've got two distinct ways of seeing: objects (*who/what*) and quantities (*how many, how much*).

3. WE SAW POSITION IN SPACE—THE *WHERE*

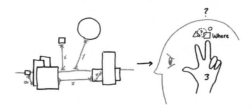

Meanwhile, a third part of our vision system was simultaneously occupied with noticing where all these objects and quantities were located, both in relation to us and in relation to one another. We saw that our friend was maybe twenty feet ahead of us and toward the right, for example, and that the dog was at our friend's foot level, but just beyond. We saw that the baby carriage was way over there to the left, and the bird was another twenty or thirty feet past that.

We also saw that all these objects were solidly attached to the earth, and that even though they were all grounded on the same horizontal plane, we had no trouble noticing what was in front of what, what was next to what, and we could even estimate the distances between everything.

Instantly recognizing these objects' positions in space was entirely distinct from simultaneously recognizing the objects. The nearest person to us may have been our friend, but her proximity had no bearing on her being our friend: She would have been the same friend even if she'd been the character farthest away. Likewise, the fact that there was a good distance between the dog and the bird didn't alter the fact that one was a bird and the other was not.

Our minds were completely capable of seeing the *who* simultaneously and yet independently of the *where,* and it turns out that that's not just academically interesting; it's actually the way we're neurologically wired. Studies in neurobiology over the past few years have revealed that two vastly different pathways in our brain's vision system account for identifying objects' positions and for identifying the objects themselves.

The first pathway has been given the wonderfully descriptive (and thankfully unscientific) name "the *where* pathway," and it identifies the parts of our brain that help us visually determine our own spatial orientation and the position of objects around us. Much of this visual processing takes place in an evolutionarily ancient part of our brain known as the reptilian brain, or brain stem, and much of the processing—if we recall the precognitive attributes we discussed in the previous chapter—takes place long before we have any conscious awareness of even knowing *what* we're looking at.

The second pathway, which has the equally descriptive name "the *what* pathway," is composed of visual processing centers located in the evolutionarily newer outer layers of our brain known as the neocortex. The *what* pathway—not surprisingly—is responsible for identifying things and attaching names to them.*

We've accounted for three independent yet interrelated ways of seeing: *who/what, how much,* and *where.* We're halfway done. Did you notice how the *ways of seeing* correspond to the 6 W's? That relationship is going to continue for the remaining three, but with a slight difference: While the first three ways of seeing are instantaneous, the next three depend on the passage of time.

4. WE SAW POSITION IN TIME—THE *WHEN*

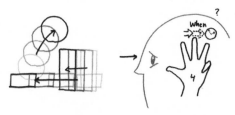

As we let our scene play out, our characters and objects moved about. Our friend walked a little, the dog jumped more, and the bird may have flown away entirely. We know this

---

* There are several theories as to why the visual processing of *where* and *what* are not only physically remote from each other in our brains, but are also separated by several million years of neurobiological evolution. See Appendix A: The Science of Visual Thinking.

because while the various parts of our vision system were working on *what* we were seeing, *how many* there were, and *where* they were, yet another part (or perhaps several parts—nobody is entirely sure how this neurologically happens) was keeping track of the objects and their positions as they moved over time. In the case of the baby carriage for example, at the beginning of our exercise we saw it in one place, but by the end it was in a different place: Over the couple minutes' time of the exercise, it had changed location. And yet our eyes didn't question whether it was a different carriage just because at one point in time it was *here* and at another point in time it was *there*. We knew it was the same carriage because our eyes knew that we were literally seeing time pass by.

Had we observed for several more minutes, we would have seen the carriage visually change in other ways. It would have become smaller as it moved farther away, it would have changed shape as its angle from our eyes shifted, and if we'd been able to watch for a really long time, it might even have changed color as its paint faded in the sun. But no matter how long we watched—as long as we stayed on the scene—we'd still see it as the *same* carriage.

Seeing the *when* is different from the three ways we've already discussed. While we saw the *who/what, how much,* and *where* instantly, to see *when* demands that at least some time pass. As obvious as that sounds, it's an important idea that has real ramifications for how we see and represent things that change over time. We can (and often do) make immediate visual judgments about objects, number, and spatial position, but we can't do the same when it comes to how things change. To see *when,* we have to see at least two different points in time—*before* and *after, now* and *then, yesterday* and *today,* etc.

5. WE SAW INFLUENCE AND CAUSE AND EFFECT—THE *HOW*

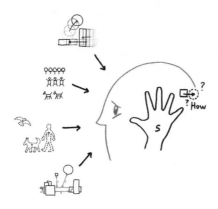

Up to this point, the four ways of seeing have been largely independent. Our eyes saw and processed *who* and *what* separately from *where* and *when*. But as we watched our scene unwind over time and saw our characters and objects shift their positions in space, something else happened: We started to see chains of related events and the impact of one thing upon another. In other words, we saw *how*. If our friend's dog lunged toward the bird, any of several things could have occurred. Perhaps our friend yanked the leash and caught the dog up short; perhaps the dog snapped our friend forward; perhaps the dog bolted, leaving our friend in the dust.

No matter what took place, we saw cause and effect in action: The dog did something (ran, barked, jumped) that forced our friend to do something in response (fall down, yell at the dog, jump even farther). Our eyes saw all of this and compared it to what we expected would happen—based on similar cause-and-effect scenes we'd seen in the past—and confirmed that the world still made sense. In the unlikely event that the dog suddenly sprouted wings and flew or our friend teleported to the other side of the park, our eyes would have been very surprised, and we would have had to reassess how our world works.

Like *when*, seeing *how* requires the passage of time, long enough for at least a little cause and effect to be visible. But unlike the other ways of seeing, *how* isn't something we distinctly see on its own. *Hows* are usually combinations of *whos*, *whats*, *how muchs*, *wheres*, and *whens* all rolled up together. In other words, the first four W's serve as the raw materials that we build together in order to see *how* things happen.

Our eyes visually deduce *how* by observing the interactions of the first four W's.

This means that of the five ways we've covered so far, *hows* are the most challenging to see: They don't appear immediately, and they require that we see (and visually combine) at least two or more of the previous W's first. We'll come back to this point several more times as we apply all this to real problem solving, but first we've got one more way to see.

6. WE SAW ALL OF THIS COME TOGETHER AND "KNEW" SOMETHING ABOUT OUR SCENE—THE *WHY*

Friends, dogs, baby carriages, birds, objects, positions, locations, changes over time, influences, causes and effects: For a simple exercise that took just a few minutes, we certainly saw a lot. And by seeing the objects, measuring their attributes and numbers, determining their position and size, tracking countless changes to them over time, and detecting interactions between them, we came to know something about our world. In fact, we've started down the path of seeing *why*.

Perhaps we don't yet know from our little scene precisely why birds fly away from dogs or not, or why a leash is an effective way of keeping a dog from crashing into a baby carriage, but given what we've seen, we won't be able to stop ourselves from making some guesses. Whether those guesses will turn out to be right or wrong will be answered only by observing similar scenes over and over, and seeing if they end up the same way.

But the truly amazing part of our vision system is how often our guesses turn out to be right. Bird-dog drills are entering our eyes every second of every waking moment, and it's staggering how rarely we make a mistake in keeping track of the *whos, whats, wheres,* etc. Most of us would probably struggle to recall times when we fundamentally misidentified someone or something, profoundly confused the positions of objects in space, or saw time flow in the wrong direction. It's not that these things can't happen; it's just that if they do, we become intensely aware of them, since they run counter to what we know. They mess up our understanding of *why*.

BACK TO THE BIRD

This wraps up our exercise on the six ways we see, except for one last thing: the bird. When we ended the exercise, I asked, "Is the bird still on the ground or did it fly away?" While I have no idea where your bird ended up, I do know this: After going through the bird-dog drill with hundreds of people, I've seen a pretty consistent two-to-one split. Two-thirds of bird-dog participants say the bird flew away—usually because it got scared by the dog—while one-third say the bird stayed on the ground—either because the exercise ended before the bird noticed the dog, or because the bird was bigger than the dog and would have been happy to eat that puppy for breakfast.

Wherever your bird ended up, the final point of the exercise is the same: Based solely on things we saw, we can begin to make rational arguments about why particular things happened in our world, and back up those arguments by pulling from the 6 W's. Whether we come away believing that birds fly away from dogs or not, we've justified and solidified our understanding of the *hows* and *whys* of the world, simply by seeing the *whos*, *whats*, *wheres*, and *whens*.

Putting the Six Ways to Work

When we *see* problems according to the 6 W's, we're taking advantage of the way our eyes and mind naturally view the world. By seeing a problem as six individual yet related components, we've got a problem-solving approach that is entirely intuitive (since it mirrors the way our eyes already see) and powerful (since it's usually a lot easier to address a handful of small challenges than one big one).

The Chocolate War

All it usually takes to see a problem clearly is to consciously seek out the 6 W's. A couple years ago, I worked with the training and personal development manager at one of the world's largest online stores. Lila had been with the company since day one and had seen it grow from a shop of twenty people to well over a thousand, and as training manager, Lila knew every one of them. Ask her a *who, what, where, when,* or *why* about anybody, and she could answer. Over her five years with the company, Lila had become an irreplaceable business asset, the one person who knew everyone, and her managers agreed that they'd bend over backward to keep her.

But one day Lila got a call from a headhunter with an offer that no amount of executive back bending could counter: chocolate. One of the nation's most highly regarded luxury chocolate brands was shifting into growth mode. All around the country, sales of high-end chocolate were up as Americans' tastes became more refined, and the company realized that if it was ever going to expand its small base of regional shops into a nationwide chain, the time was now. But in spite of the need for speed, the company's leaders made the decision that growth would not come at the cost of quality.

Which meant that everyone involved in opening the new stores—from the managers to the chocolatiers to the cashiers—would need quality-oriented and quality-centric training, and lots of it. The company needed a training manager with experience in rapidly growing organizations, which meant that the company needed someone like Lila. And Lila, tasting a real opportunity, realized that she was more ready for a change than she'd thought. She took the job.

When Lila met her new team, she was awed by their experience and dedication. Most had been with the company for the bulk of their careers and knew exactly how things worked, inside and out. This was good for Lila, because it meant she'd have the collected insight in the company available to her as she ramped up the new training engine. But it also turned out to be bad for Lila because it meant that her people had been looking at their same materials for so long that they could no longer see them.

When Lila asked for a sample of existing training materials, her team brought her hundreds of documents in dozens of binders, each with cryptic names: LLT v.12, CTFS&C 2005, and ISMT Lvl 2 (SM) (*Leader-Lead Training, Chocolate Tasting for Staff and Customers, In-Store Management Training for Shift Mgrs*). When she asked for an overview to orient herself within these unfamiliar terms, her team came back with another dozen documents: calendars and schedules, org structures and job titles, training locations, lists of desired outcomes, and test result summaries.

Her team didn't "get" what Lila was asking for, and Lila wasn't "getting" what she wanted. For her, it was like looking under the hood and not seeing anything useful: There were too many pieces with too few visible connections to discern any patterns. There was no question that her team knew what they were talking about; they answered any query from Lila with speed and confidence. When Lila asked, "Who attends Leader-Lead Training version 12?" they all answered in unison, "All new hires who have completed Bean Basics but have not yet qualified on customer tastings management."

It drove Lila crazy: Her people knew their training programs so well that they couldn't remember what it was like to *not* know them. Since the curriculum had grown around them, her team couldn't see training as anything but a fully integrated piece—which was the last thing that Lila could discern. As an experienced trainer herself, Lila knew that the fix relied at least as much on her as on her team. They knew what was what but couldn't describe it; she didn't know what was what and couldn't see anything.

Lila had three choices: She could bear all the pain (attend the entire training series herself—a minimum eighteen-week commitment, normally spread out over five plus years); she could make her team bear all the pain (by telling them to go off as a group and not come back until they'd rewritten everything in a way that could be summarized in an hour); or they could all share the pain.

Lila chose the shared-pain option, and that's when she called me. She wanted to arrange a whiteboarding session to which everybody brought all their training materials, looked for connections with everybody else's materials, and kept at it until all the pieces gelled into visible alignment. Not being a fan of day-long "brainstorming sessions," Lila wondered if I had any ideas about how pictures might minimize the pain.

I suggested that she and her team lay everything out and then work through it piece by piece, trying to *see* the chocolate training process as it is reflected across the 6 W's.

1. Looking over all the materials in front of them, I suggested that they try to see the *who* and the *what* of the training system.

- *Who* gets trained and w*ho* does the training?
- *What* topics are taught and w*hat* lessons are presented?

2. Next, try to see *how much* and *how many*.

- *How many* lessons are required; *how much* time do they take?
- *How many* people can attend each lesson; *how many* instructors are needed?

3. Next, try to see the *where*.

- Geographically, *where* do the lessons take place: in-store, training facilities, at home?
- Conceptually, *where* do the lessons overlap in content, structure, or attendance?

4. Then the *when*.

- *When* do the lessons take place?
- In *what sequence* do they need to occur?

5. Then the *how*.

- *How* does one lesson relate to another; *how* do they fit together?
- *How* are the lessons taught: face-to-face, in a group, online?
- *How* are the lessons applied; *how* do you know you're ready to move on?

6. Finally, try to see the *why*.

- *Why* is training necessary; w*hy* make the effort at all?
- *Why* judge, *why* test, *why* track, *why* follow through?

Then I suggested that as they *see* these things, they map them on the whiteboard according to the 6 W's categories. Lila thought that sounded fine and asked me to join in. I did, and here is what I saw on the table when I arrived:

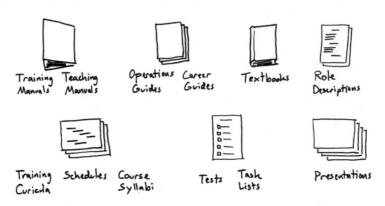

Training Manuals Teaching Manuals Operations Guides Career Guides Textbooks Role Descriptions

Training Curicula Schedules Course Syllabi Tests Task Lists Presentations

Who

Execs

Store Managers

Shift Managers

Factory Staff Retail Staff

Here we see *who* needs to be trained, from staff to executives.

The Chocolate Training Process as Seen According to the 6 W's

First off, we looked through the training materials with an eye toward seeing which people were involved. Each time we came across a role, job title, or position, we wrote it down. There were a lot of specifics, so we decided to summarize them by organizational level. This turned out to be a good way to start, since everyone in the room already had a common understanding of how the organization was structured, making it easy to capture the basics.

Next, we looked for specifics describing what was taught. This was a little harder, not only because the list was long, but because different trainers thought about courses in different ways. Some summarized by teacher, some by materials, others by outcome. After a brief discussion, we agreed to make our list based on *what* specifically was taught, which led to the emergence of a fairly natural set of categories. Even at this early point in the day, there was a shared sense of accomplishment in generating a single list that everyone could see and agree on.

What

Factory Training

Bean Basics

- Cacao Essentials
- Bean Selection
- Bean Preparation

Manufacturing Processes

- Roasting
- Grinding + Mixing
- Tempering
- Packaging Essentials

Advanced Chocolatier

- Advanced Flavors
- Advanced Packaging
- Sustainability

Retail Training

Retail Essentials

- Sales Essentials
- Customer Relations
- Operating Essentials

Advanced Retail

- Tastings
- Special Events

Manager Training

Retail Management

- Advanced Ops
- Financial Essentials
- Marketing 101
- People Development
- Global Sourcing + Impacts

Here we see *what* the employees are being trained on, from chocolate manufacturing and retail basics up to advanced business management courses.

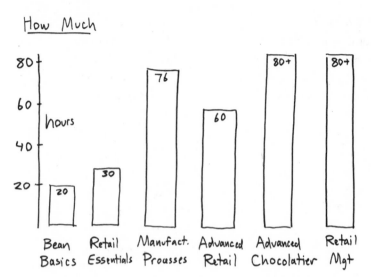

How Much

hours

20	30	76	60	80+	80+
Bean Basics	Retail Essentials	Manufact. Prousses	Advanced Retail	Advanced Chocolatier	Retail Mgt

Here we see *how much* training is required, and that the hours increase as people become more expert and have more to learn.

Where

Factory Retail Stores Home

Here we see *where* training takes place, from factory training to home learning.

When we came to how much training was required, it was difficult to separate out the specifics. It depended on the subject, the audience, previous experience, etc. But since we'd just created a shared list of *whats,* we had a common base from which to start. So we took the top categories from the *what* map and estimated total training hours associated with each.

Seeing the geographic *wheres* was a no-brainer since there were only three physical places that anyone could think of where training took place. It offered a nice rest and we all took a breather . . . until we started in on the conceptual side of *where.* When we started to discuss such ideas as where the courses overlapped in terms of content or audience, or where they mapped on various career paths, the going got tougher. Not wanting to lose momentum, we decided to press on with the *whens* and come back later.

It was a good decision to make: As we mapped out *when* the various courses needed to be taken, another natural pattern emerged. It turned out that there wasn't a single timeline, but rather two: the path for employees entering the factory and the path for employees entering the retail side of the business. Both took the same amount of time to complete, but both were completely distinct from each other—which effectively accounted for the course overlap challenge we'd hit a few minutes before. In this case, by seeing *when*, we resolved the issue of *where*.

Then we took a break.

It turned out that the break was a good idea, too, since mapping out the *how* proved to be the most difficult. This wasn't surprising since we know that *how* is fundamentally the intersection of all the previous W's. Since we'd spent all morning on the *who, what, how much, where,* and *when,* we were able to finally nail down a model of *how* training worked that, again, everyone could see and agree with.

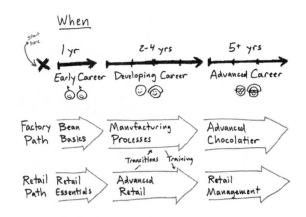

Here we see *when* training occurs throughout the entire career of the chocolatier, and for the first time we see that there are, in fact, two different timelines.

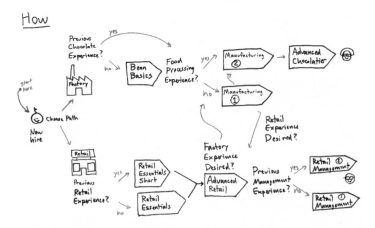

Here we see *how* training takes place, and we see that the two different paths have options based on previous experience and individual career choices.

Why

Last, we see *why* training takes place: to make the best chocolate in the world, and to make sure the largest number of chocolate lovers possible can get some.

Seeing the *why* was a good way to end the day. Everyone knew exactly why all this training was needed—to provide a way for a lot of people to start making, selling, and enjoying really good chocolate without sacrificing quality.

Who, what, how much, where, when, how, and *why:* For the first time, everyone saw eye to eye. Lila saw why it had been so difficult for her team to summarize everything (there were a lot of pieces here) and the team saw why she needed a summary (in order to see how to optimize and grow the training process). In one day, we'd managed to convert hundreds of pages and many years of experience into a handful of pictures. Now Lila could see what her team was talking about, and they could see what she was after.

Lila still had an enormous amount to learn from her people, and she faced the even larger task of finding a way to scale up all this training in order to support hundreds of new people, but her new career in chocolate finally felt under control. Now she could see where she was going.

Preview of Coming Attractions: Get Ready for the Six Ways of Showing

There is another way to use these six ways. Because they encapsulate all the ways we see, they also encapsulate all the ways we can *show*. When the time comes to move to the final step in the visual thinking process, we're going to come back to these same six. But next time, we won't be using the 6 W's as ways of seeing, we'll be using them as the basis for showing other people what we've seen, and thus completing the visual thinking cycle.

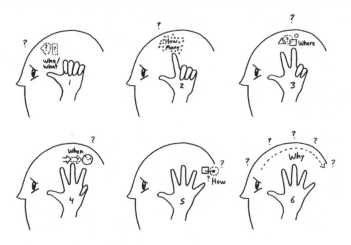

The six ways we see: who/what, how many, where, when, how, and why:

But we're not quite there yet. So far, we've been focused on our *eyes* and looking and seeing—the tools and steps that we rely on to process visual information from the outside world. In the next chapter, we're going to close our eyes and start spinning all those visual inputs around, manipulating them, turning them upside down, and trying to create entirely new patterns. We're going to turn on our *mind's eye* and start *imagining*.

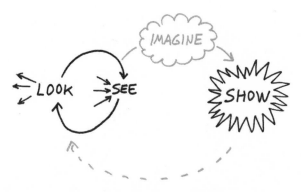

Everything we've seen up till now is going to come back around when it's time to show:

CHAPTER 6

THE SQUID: A PRACTICAL LESSON IN APPLIED IMAGINATION

Seeing with Our Eyes Closed: The Art of Imagining

U p to this point, our eyes have been our windows on the world: Through *active looking* we used our eyes to collect visual information about the challenges in front of us, and through careful *seeing* we broke that incoming information into six different visual types. But as useful as our eyes have been, we're now going to leave them behind. In this section, we're going to be seeing in ways that don't require our eyes at all; what we will require is our ability to *imagine*.

Imagining is how we let our mind's eye take over so that we can see things that aren't physically visible in front of us. This means taking the concrete coordinates, patterns, and components that we see in the world and translating them into abstract pictures that we can manipulate inside our heads.

Imagining isn't a magical process that requires us to enter a trancelike state or visualize positive energy or anything equally disconcerting to most businesspeople. Imagining is simply another approach to seeing, and in most respects it is not far removed from the six ways of seeing we've already discussed. The only real difference is that when we imagine, we're letting our mind's eye see things that aren't actually there. When we imagine, we're using the same high-level mental vision processing centers that we do when our eyes are open. We're just letting our mind's eye do the visual cooking instead of ordering in.

From a business problem-solving perspective, imagining is an extraordinarily powerful way of conjuring up ideas and solutions, and there are dozens of approaches, exercises, and books available for improving the creative thinking process. Some, like visual memory games, mind mapping, visual analogies and metaphors—yes, even specific kinds of meditation—can be applied with great success to the visual thinking process.

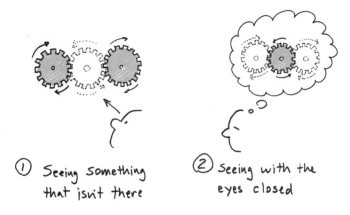

① Seeing something that isn't there

② Seeing with the eyes closed

The best way to see something that *isn't* there is to look with our eyes closed, and that's where *imagining* comes in.

Since excellent descriptions of many of these are available elsewhere,* we're going to focus on a single imagining framework that I call the SQVID. The SQVID (we'll get to the origin of the name in a moment) is a visual imagination activation tool that I rely on constantly when I'm working with clients. Like the other visual thinking tools, the SQVID is a stand-alone exercise that can to be used anytime, anywhere to fully engage our visual imaginations. As we'll see, the SQVID simultaneously helps us complete two critical tasks of imagining: It activates every corner of our mind's eye to fully realize a mental image, and it helps us see that image through the eyes of our potential audience.

The Many Ways to Slice an Apple

The best way to introduce the SQVID is with another visualization exercise. (Ironically, this time I'd rather you didn't close your eyes.) But instead of sitting on a park bench, we're going to travel farther from home: This time imagine that you're on vacation on a tropical South Sea island, and on a gorgeous sunny day you're taking a leisurely stroll along the beach. On one side of you is white sand and turquoise ocean. On the other side is deep jungle, blooming with tall palms and colorful plants. Got it? Not too hard to conjure up that scene, I hope.

---

* See Appendix B: Resources for Visual Thinkers.

Now imagine that as you stroll along, you meet a local islander coming the other way, eating an unusual purple fruit. Although you don't speak the local language, this is a very friendly island, and the islander nods hello. You nod back, and the islander stops and hands you one of the strange purple fruits, indicating that you should taste it. You accept and take a tentative chomp. Hmm . . . it's really good, almost like an apple, only sweeter and juicier.

The villager doesn't seem to be in any hurry to go anywhere, and you've got nothing pressing to do, so you decide to reciprocate by sharing something about apples back home. Of course, there's nothing around that looks like an apple, so the language barrier dictates that you'll have to use pictures. Luckily, you have several cocktail napkins from your resort and a felt-tip pen in your pocket. As you pull out these excellent visual thinking tools, you begin to imagine the best way to visually describe an apple.

Your first sketch is a simple little drawing of an apple, the first thing that pops into your mind's eye.

But, thinking about this sketch and noting the lush jungle around you, you realize that perhaps it makes more sense to elaborate a bit and add an apple tree.

Then again, maybe it's better to show the whole orchard.

Odd: All three of the drawings are valid descriptions of apples, yet each looks different—and this is just the beginning. Now that you're thinking about it, you realize that depending on what you most want the islander to understand about apples, you could sketch all sorts of other views.

You might wish to try to describe the apple in all its luscious glory: red and shiny, round and shapely.

Or if you'd like to share why an apple a day keeps the doctor away, you might wish to show how nutritious an apple is.

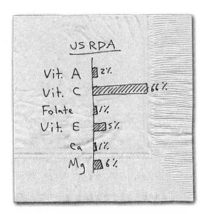

You might wish to share your idea of apple perfection, the apple pie.

Or you might find it more useful to explain how to make that perfect apple pie.

You might wish to show the apple all by itself, the better to point out specific details of the fruit.

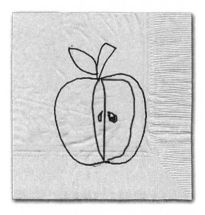

Or maybe it makes more sense to compare the apple to other fruits that the islander may already know.

You could show how an apple begins.

Or you could show how the apple ends.

Wow! All that from one apple? Believe it or not, standing there on the beach with nothing but a pen, a napkin, and an islander looking at you, you've activated every corner of your mind's eye and both sides of your brain. From an imagining perspective, you've taken a single simple starting idea—apple—and let your mind's eye run wild with it, conjuring up views, aspects, and details you might never have thought of if you'd been able to get away with, "Yep. Tastes like an apple."

At the same time you were tossing this apple around in your head, you were also beginning to think about how—in this particular circumstance and to this particular audience—to visually describe your apple so that it would make the most sense to the islander. In other words, you were starting to think about your own idea from your audience's perspective, recognizing that in other circumstances there might be better or different ways to draw it.

OK, let's step off the beach and back to reality for a moment. Since I know this is going to come up (it always does), I'm going to address something that you might be thinking. If we'd just gone through this exercise in a workshop, guaranteed somebody would say, "Now, wait a minute. You told us we're dealing with a local islander, and yet here we're sketching out nutritional breakdowns and apple pie cooking instructions. That's silly. The islander isn't going to care about that."

To which I say, "Possibly, but I never told you what the islander looked like. If he or she was wearing a grass skirt, perhaps the first picture might be the best. But what if this islander was wearing a lab coat and had a stethoscope around his or her neck? Or what if he or she was wearing a baker's hat? Which apple pictures would be better then?"

And that's really the second point of the exercise—to recognize that even if we have only one seemingly simple idea to share, there are always many ways to show it to our audience, and some are far more appropriate and effective than others. That's why tossing this apple back and forth is both a great way to force our mind's eye into looking at our idea in multiple ways (always discovering something new as we do) and to start thinking about what's going to be the best way—from our audience's point of view—to eventually show it.

Enter the SQVID: The Full-Brain Visual Workout

What we just went through on the beach was the SQVID exercise. At its most basic level, the SQVID is just a series of five questions that we walk our initial idea through in order to bring it to visual clarity and to refine its focus—both according to what's most important to us and what's most important to our audience. The SQVID helps us imagine what visual messages we'd like to convey *before* we start worrying about which picture we're going to draw.

The word SQVID is a simple mnemonic composed of the first letter of the first word of the same five questions that we tossed around back there on the beach. (Note: the *V* is taken from the Roman *U,* and the *D* is from the Greek for *delta,* the symbol of change. So we could say this is both a multilingual and a classical SQVID.☺)

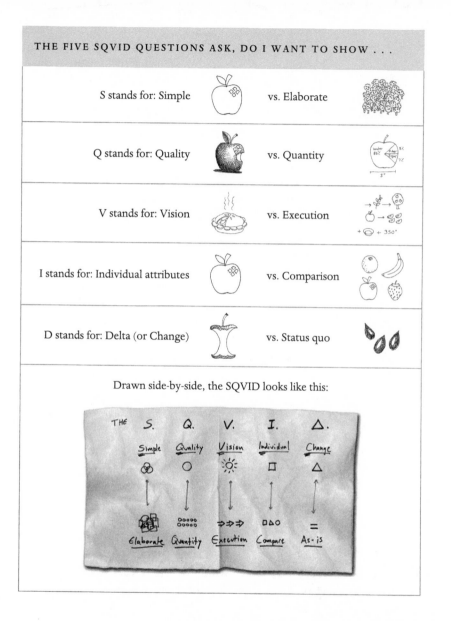

S stands for: Simple		vs. Elaborate
Q stands for: Quality		vs. Quantity
V stands for: Vision		vs. Execution
I stands for: Individual attributes		vs. Comparison
D stands for: Delta (or Change)		vs. Status quo

Drawn side-by-side, the SQVID looks like this:

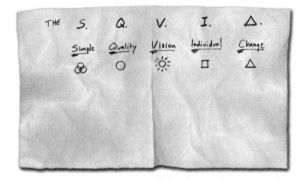

There are two main ways to use the SQVID, both simple and insightful. The first—as we did on the beach—is to walk through the five questions in order and think of how we could visually describe our idea according to each option: a *simple* view or an *elaborate* view, a *qualitative* view or a *quantitative* view, etc. Then, either on paper or just in our mind's eye, draw out what each view might look like.

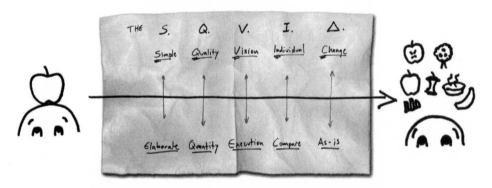

SQVID pathway 1: By walking our idea through the five questions and coming up with a visual description for each end, we force our mind's eye to come up with at least ten different views.

As we've seen, this pathway through the SQVID forces our visual system to switch gears back and forth as we move from question to question, extreme to extreme. (Try it: I swear you can literally feel your mind's eye grinding metal as it jumps from quantitative visual description to visionary visual description and so on. It's a trip.) This shifting of gears in turn exercises corners of our mind's eye we rarely explore, forcing us to conjure up images that we rarely think of. This pathway is ideal for generating an unexpectedly broad number of ways to visually represent our idea, and leaves us with many views to choose from when it comes time to pick which to show.

The second pathway through the SQVID is driven less by our idea and more by our anticipated audience's expectations. In this approach, we use the SQVID like a graphic equalizer, identifying which overall "settings" are most useful to our audience, regardless of the details of what we're going to describe. For example, we may know that whenever we need to share any idea with our company's project managers, we should skew toward quantitative, execution-oriented visuals, but if we'll be talking with the press, we may want to skew toward simple visionary representations.

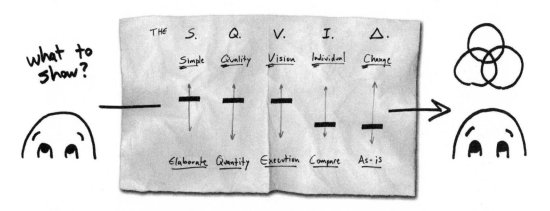

SQVID pathway 2: By setting the graphic equalizer sliders toward the views we think will be most relevant to our audience, we provide focus on which type of picture will be best to show them.

Either way we walk through the SQVID (idea focusing or audience focusing), a pattern emerges between the upper and lower extremes of the SQVID that will prove useful for really pushing our thinking—and for addressing an eternal conflict in business problem solving. On the upper part of each slider we see simplicity, quality, vision, individuality, and change. These skew toward what are typically considered creative attributes: the descriptive, the synthetic, the different, the abstract, attributes that are difficult to measure and carry more emotional weight. We'll call the top the "warm" side of the equalizer.

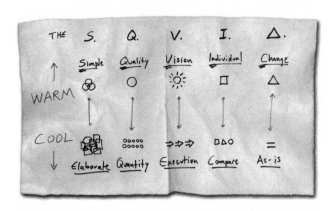

Attributes on the top of the SQVID are "warm" or "right brain": simple, qualitative, visionary, etc. Those on the bottom are "cool" or "left brain": complex, quantitative, execution oriented, etc.

When we look at the lower extreme of each slider—complexity, quantity, execution, comparison, and the status quo—we see alignment toward the more traditional notions of business attributes—attributes that are numeric, analytic, detailed, factual, and measurable. Because these are more rational and detached from emotional associations, we'll call the bottom side of the equalizer the "cool" side.

In other words, by forcing ourselves to look at our idea from every point on the SQVID, a fascinating thing happens, with an equally fascinating outcome: We fully activate both the left ("analytic") and right ("creative") sides of our brain.* This means that if we're the kind of person who thrives on detailed quantitative analysis of problems, using

---

* For more on the basics of the right-brain/left-brain split, see Appendix A: The Science of Visual Thinking.

the SQVID activates both our more familiar thinking style and the creative side that we don't see so much. Conversely, if we consider ourselves as more visionary or qualitative, using the SQVID gets us to work out the kinks on our more analytic side.

This means that the SQVID serves as an excellent way to get groups of businesspeople who might rarely understand one another's points of view to begin to see eye to eye.

FOR RIGHTBRAINERS	FOR LEFTBRAINERS
When the creatively inclined need to deal with those hard-nosed business types:	*When the business inclined need to deal with those squishy, abstract, creative people:*
One benefit of the SQVID is that by creating a structured and repeatable way of using our abilities to imagine, the approach illustrates in a concrete way the importance of looking at both warm/creative and cool/business attributes when thinking through an idea.	One benefit of the SQVID is that by visually defining the interplay of both the emotional and the rational when imagining an idea, it intuitively and conceptually illustrates the need to balance creative visioning with practical business considerations.
So, when facing a dubious business type as you describe the value of your simple, qualitative, visionary, individualistic and industry changing idea, show them how it fits into the rationality of the SQVID.	So when facing a dubious creative type when you need to share the value of your complex, quantitative, execution-oriented comparison of present-day realities, show then how it fits into the creativity of the SQVID.

The SQVID in Action

As pleasant as it is to imagine ourselves on that beach drawing pictures of apples, a far more likely scenario will find us running into a coworker at the water cooler, meeting with an employee in cubicle land, or preparing to give a presentation to the board of directors in the conference room. And while we're probably not going to need to describe an apple, we will need to describe just exactly what it is that we are working on.

To see how we can use the SQVID's five questions to help focus our visual ideas, let's take a look at how others have approached answering them. The rest of this chapter takes each of the five questions and shows how they were visually addressed by real people, in all cases business professionals with no formal training in the visual arts.

QUESTION 1: SIMPLE OR ELABORATE?

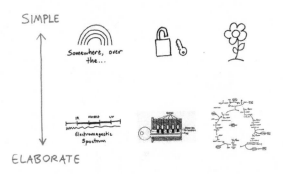

When I introduce the SQVID as a visual thinking tool and talk about the first question, someone always asks, "Isn't 'complex' the opposite of 'simple?'" And for that matter, if the idea of pictures is to clarify communications, why would anyone ever want to intentionally show complexity?"

This is an excellent question itself because it demands two important but subtle answers. First, the opposite of "simple" is not "complex," but rather "elaborate." The Möbius strip, a continuous ribbon that is folded over so that mathematically speaking it has only one side, is a perfect example of something that is both complex and simple at the same time.

Second, this is not just a minor point of semantics: It cuts right to the heart of solving problems with pictures. One of the most important virtues of visual thinking is its ability to clarify things so that the complex can be better understood, but that does not mean that all good visual thinking is about simplification. *The real goal of visual thinking is to make the complex understandable by making it visible—not by making it simple.* Whether that goal demands a simple picture, an elaborate one, or an intentionally complex one is almost always determined by the audience and its familiarity with the subject being addressed.

Let's look at the recent work of Jeff Hawkins, an engineer who invented the PalmPilot and founded Handspring, and who has spent the last several years becoming an expert in the study of the human brain, especially the neocortex.

While his new company, Numenta, focuses on mimicking the behavior of the neocortex with software, Jeff spends much of his time on the road discussing his views on how the brain works. He presents to audiences as diverse as high school–age students at New York's Juilliard School and neuroscience professors at the Massachusetts Institute of Technology.

The amazing one-sided Möbius strip: a perfect example of something simultaneously simple and complex.

Regardless of who he is talking to, Jeff gives essentially the same speech, but how he succeeds in getting his various audiences engaged is that he varies the level of simplicity versus elaboration to match the expertise of his listeners. Jeff begins his talks by showing one of two drawings of how the brain works, one for lay audiences and one for the experts. The simple picture is composed of two boxes, thirteen arrows, and eleven words, and describes conceptually how our brains process incoming information.

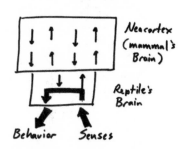

Hawkins's second drawing is also composed of boxes, arrows and text . . . just a lot more of them. This version is the one that Jeff shows when talking to neuroscientists, PhD's, and other experts. Although conceptually the same as the first drawing—the same components, the same relationships, even the same shapes—this

This is the picture Jeff Hawkins uses to introduce general audiences to his ideas.

How the Brain works:

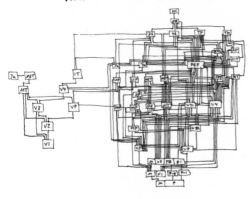

This is the drawing Hawkins shows to scientists and PhD's.

drawing scares off anyone not already an expert in brain science. At the same time, Jeff needs this drawing as his introduction when addressing the experts because if he doesn't show something this elaborate, they won't believe that he knows what he's talking about.

The most interesting part of this whole story is that by the time his presentation is over, Jeff has shown both audiences—experts and newbies—both pictures. For the lay audience, seeing the wildly complex drawing after they understand the basics of how the brain works is amazing. And the neurobiologists and PhD's get really excited by Jeff's simple drawing because once they believe he knows what he is talking about, they find the drawing refreshing.

QUESTION 2: QUALITY OR QUANTITY?

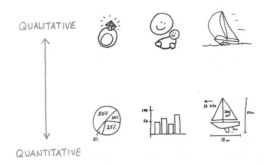

Pilots come in two types: those who fly by the seat of their pants and those who fly by the numbers. The early days of aviation were dominated by the first type—pilots feeling their aircraft's position and orientation through their butts' contact with the seat. We can think of them as "qualitative" aviators, experts at guiding their aircraft by experience, instinct, and intuition.

The second type of pilot flies in a completely different way. By-the-numbers pilots know that facts, data, and the monitoring of multiple precise measurements keep them in the air. Because these pilots know that the continuous interpretation of measured altitude, heading, airspeed, position, and orientation is what keeps them alive, we can think of them as "quantitative" aviators.

It's a rare pilot who can fly both ways, but when *Apollo 11* made the first landing on the moon in 1969, that's exactly what Commander Neil Armstrong had to do. Just above the lunar surface and with only seconds of fuel remaining for him to land, Armstrong—considered among the most by-the-numbers astronauts in NASA—saw a pile of boulders littering the planned landing spot. He did what any wide-awake driver would do when a pothole appears just ahead. He stomped on the gas and drove by the seat of his pants. After finally touching down safely on the moon's surface, *Apollo 11* Mission Control could only say, "You got a bunch of guys about to turn blue. We're breathing again. Thanks a lot."

The next time we land on the moon, Mary "Missy" Cummings is going to make sure it won't be anywhere near that exciting. Not that Missy isn't used to exciting landings. As one of the first women naval aviators to be cleared for combat flight, Missy has landed her A-4 Skyhawk countless times on tossing aircraft carrier decks. Now that she runs MIT's Humans and Automation Lab, she gets the chance to put her academic background in systems engineering and her firsthand piloting experience into practice: Her lab is designing the visual displays that the next lunar astronauts will use when they land on the moon, tentatively scheduled for 2013.

As Missy puts it, "As instrumentation designers, our biggest challenge is deciding how much

LUNAR MODULE CONTROLS AND DISPLAYS

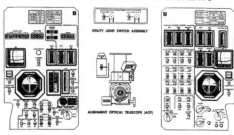

The eyes of astronauts in the 1960s had to move quickly across several differently configured instruments, burning through many "cognitive cycles" just to figure out which way they were going.

information *not* to show, and how to trick people into perceiving what we most want them to see. We do this through multivariate instrument optimization, which is a fancy way of describing the process of layering many numeric visual inputs together to create a single, rapidly perceived qualitative display." In other words, Missy's challenge is to find a visual way to merge seat-of-the-pants and by-the-numbers flying.

While 1960s-era Apollo astronauts' eyes had to jump repeatedly across many instruments to get a sense of situational awareness, the goal of Missy's team's new VAVI (Vertical Altitude and Velocity Indicator) is to provide immediate visual cues that are both numerically precise and convey directional information. Her solution was a completely new instrument with "waving arms" that help make astronauts *feel visually* whether they are going up or down while simultaneously providing the critical numeric readouts necessary for pilots to know exactly where they are and how fast they are going.

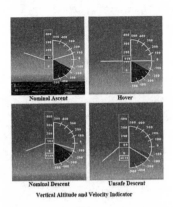

Nominal Ascent   Hover

Nominal Descent   Unsafe Descent

Vertical Altitude and Velocity Indicator

Missy's team's new VAVI design relies on "waving arms" to help astronauts visually feel their rate of ascent or descent.

Her team has tested their VAVI in a U.S. Marine Corps Harrier Jump Jet with great success, and is looking forward to pushing it out into the commercial aviation market.

Even if NASA doesn't end up heading back to the moon for a long time, Missy is pleased with what her team has accomplished. By creating a working prototype of a single dashboard instrument that provides both qualitative and quantitative information, they have learned much that can be applied toward the design of business management control panels that make today's digital dashboards look like leftovers from the early days of flight.

QUESTION 3: VISION OR EXECUTION?

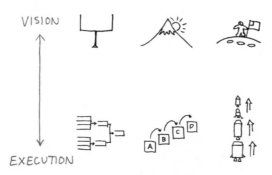

Sometimes the most important message a business audience can hear from its leaders is that "we know where we're going." Other times, all the audience needs to hear is that "we know exactly how we're going to get there." This is the difference between vision and execution, and whichever message is more important, it is often best *heard* through the eyes.

In 1992, when the soon-to-be-appointed chairman of the consulting giant Bain & Company needed to deliver a rousing message to the foundering company she was about to take over, she knew that unless she was able to immediately articulate and share a new vision for the company, poor morale would bring the once-proud firm to its knees. It was clear-eyed-vision time, and Orit Gadiesh believed she had the right vision to share.

Orit's husband was an avid sailor and frequently spoke with her about the joys and terrors of sailing solo. Among other stories of the sea, he told her about the earth's *two* north poles—something unknown to most people but a matter of life and death to sailors. There is magnetic north—which is easy to find because the needle on a compass always points toward it—and then there is true north, which is the actual point around which the earth spins. While the position of true north never varies, magnetic north moves over time and shifts position as you sail around the globe, which means that if a sailor follows only his compass, he will sooner or later get lost and wreck.

Orit saw parallels in that story with her own company, and realized that in the world of business consulting—a world influenced by short-term market changes and faddish business thinking—this model of two norths also held true: Consultants who steered only by the shifting compass of the market and fads would founder, while those who tacked to the true north of their fundamental business beliefs and culture would succeed.

As she prepared for the speech of her lifetime, this image kept coming to her mind, and she decided to gamble on it. So in August 1992, at the worst of the firm's woes, Orit got up to give her "no numbers" speech, a no-bull talk intended to establish pride and direction through the clear articulation of clear ideas. Using the simple visual of a compass pointing not straight up at magnetic north, but slightly toward the side—toward true north—Orit spoke about the need to not be swayed from the firm's founding principles.

The Bain & Company prototype logo: a compass pointing not to magnetic north, but to true north.

Orit received a standing ovation and became the only woman ever to head a major consulting company. Under her direction, the company grew 25 percent in the next five years, doubling its geographic reach. Today Bain is again considered the most innovative of the major consulting firms, and the dedication of the company's consultants is legend—and the company's logo is a compass pointing to true north.

The opposite of the "where we are going" statement of vision is the "how we are going to get there, step-by-step process" chart. Bain & Company, like any business that plans and delivers complex projects, lives by timelines and Gantt charts. Designed in the 1920s by Henry Laurence Gantt, a mechanical engineer who became one of the first of a new breed of business thinkers called management consultants, the Gantt chart is often considered one of the most important project management breakthroughs of the twentieth century.

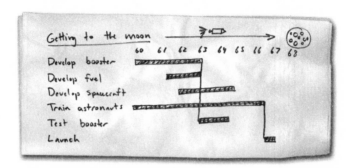

A Gantt chart is really nothing more than a bar chart laid on its side, with the length of each bar representing how long a specific task will take to complete. What makes a Gantt chart useful in showing how to get to a successful project outcome is that it *visually* shows the steps that need to take place, represents those steps in order, and clearly illustrates how any one step is dependent upon others.

Today, business software packages generate Gantt charts so easily that it is difficult for the modern consultant, project manager, technical architect, or builder to imagine a time when such visual representations didn't exist. Used on every sort of project from the Hoover Dam construction in the 1930s to the moon-landing program of the 1960s to virtually any major technology project today, the Gantt chart has stood the test of time as the way to show not *where* we're going, but *how* we're going to get there.

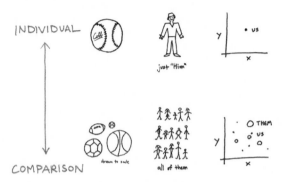

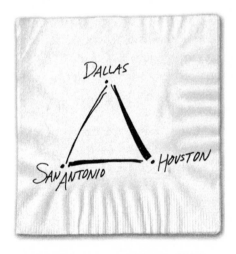

Texas's most famous napkin: Herb Kelleher and Rollin King's sketch that started Southwest Airlines.

Herb Kelleher was a lawyer from New Jersey who decided that the big open spaces of his wife's native Texas looked like a good place to set up business, so he packed up the family and headed to San Antonio.

One afternoon in 1967, Kelleher was sitting at the prestigious St. Anthony Club, helping his client Rollin King finish up the paperwork that would close Rollin's failed regional airline. But Rollin wasn't through with the airline business: He picked up a napkin and sketched a triangle on it. As he wrote SAN ANTONIO, HOUSTON, and DALLAS on one of each of three points, Rollin explained another crazy airline idea to Herb—an idea that four years later became Southwest Airlines.

Rather than running a small airline that serviced small towns, why not run a small airline that serviced big cities—the three biggest boomtowns in Texas, in fact? Because it flew to only three cities, the airline would not come under the regulation of the Texas Civil Aeronautics Board, thus freeing it to financially operate pretty much as it pleased. And by flying to Dallas's otherwise deserted Love Field, it would offer a far easier commute for Dallas-based business travelers.

Southwest legend says that Herb agreed with Rollin on two things: first, that the idea was crazy, and second, that the idea was brilliant. On its own, their simple map illustrated the fundamental operating principles of the company that Herb and Rollin agreed to start that evening: fly short routes between busy cities, avoid hubs, and where possible fly into smaller, secondary airfields. One napkin; one good idea; one profitable airline.

But where that napkin really made an impression was when it was compared to the route maps of the big airlines of the day—American, Continental, and Braniff. Seeing them now side by side shows even more clearly why this plan was destined to succeed.

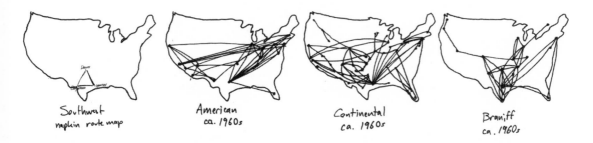

Perhaps it's not surprising why Southwest's plan worked: When compared to its competitors' routes, it looks like three strokes of genius.

In 1967, as we've said, the biggest airlines flying in and out of Texas all operated according to the "hub and spoke" model of air transport, which offered the airlines the most convenient way to move the maximum number of passengers. By delivering passengers from many spokes to a central hub, then flying them out on another spoke, the airlines could avoid the difficulties associated with operating countless direct flights between cities. While this model worked well for the airlines and for passengers traveling long distances, it was not at all convenient for local, shorter distance air travel.

Although it took four years of legal wrangling by Herb to get started, by 1971 Southwest was in the air. By focusing only on a small group of cities, Southwest was able to combine operating efficiencies with a convenience and price that Texas-based businessmen found highly desirable. That, combined with gung-ho marketing that included hot-pants-wearing stewardesses and "free" fifths of Chivas for passengers who purchased full-fare tickets, ensured that Southwest soon became the airline to beat on domestic routes, a legacy that has been proven in thirty years of unbroken profitability, an otherwise unheard of record in aviation.

QUESTION 5: THE WAY THINGS ARE VERSUS THE WAY THEY COULD BE

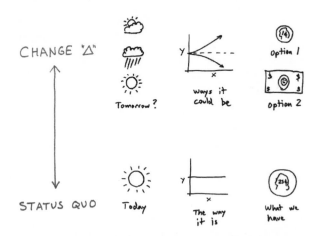

A recent work efficiency study conducted inside one of America's largest banks revealed an unsettling number: The constant communications enabled through e-mail, instant messaging, Web-based tools, conference calling, and video conferences left senior managers with an average of only four minutes to spend on any given task before being interrupted. The data was only slightly better for executive vice presidents and VPs, directors, and staff. Everyone at the bank was feeling as if they were slipping further and further behind on what they needed to get done, while simultaneously they saw that their stack of to-dos just kept growing.

Seeing the numbers, the bank knew it had to act, and fast. If the highest paid decision makers couldn't spend more than four minutes without interruption, how could they possibly take the time to make good decisions? A small SWAT team of internal thought leaders was called together to see what could be done. Sitting in a room with a whiteboard, the team was quickly able to visually show the problems.

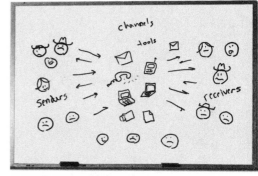

Status quo: The bank's SWAT team sketched out the company's time crisis.

The simple sketch showed the world in which the bank employees lived "today." For very good reasons, the bank had cultivated an environment where open communications was valued above almost all else. Letting branch managers speak directly to senior managers allowed regional issues to be resolved quickly.

But instead of employees being happy that they could always reach out to one another, message overload caused many people to give up on answering *any* device. Of course that wasn't possible either—among all the noise there was still a tremendous amount of valuable information being shared.

Sometimes a clear articulation of the status quo is all that a project needs to get it moving. But not this time: The SWAT team realized that if they couldn't come up with some way to address this problem, it was unlikely that anyone further up in management could either. They hadn't been called together just to say "we know what is wrong." They knew they needed to find an answer.

They started by imagining what things would look like when they had succeeded—when people could communicate with whomever they needed to whenever they needed to, and at the same time the receiver could choose when and how to be notified of the incoming messages.

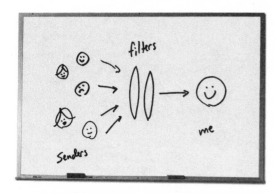

The team then created a view of what the perfect world might look like: everything filtered by sender, priority, urgency, and personal preferences.

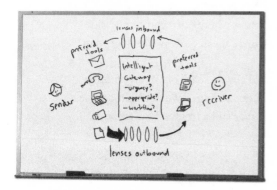

On the second pass of "what might be," the team got to a more realistic solution: inbound and outbound filters.

The team was happy with that. Although it did nothing to address *how*, it at least showed the situation they'd like to have, and served as a starting point for imagining a better future. Then it dawned on the team that they may have gone too far in putting themselves into the picture. They had become so defensive about their own time and keeping a filter on what was coming *in* that they forgot to think about how to send information back *out*.

So they took another pass at their picture, this time recognizing that every sender is also a receiver, and that the receiver—if he or she wishes to have incoming communications filtered by urgency, relevance to a specific project, and overall importance—must then also take responsibility for indicating those same criteria in messages he or she sends out.

Senders and receivers sit on either side of a set of lenses that filter according to a whole range of criteria, some filtering messages on the way in and some on the way out. "Channels" (phone, e-mail, IM, mail) become secondary to the type of message itself, and can be chosen by either sender or receiver, depending on their preferences.

Now the team agreed that they had a model for what to aim for. It was still highly conceptual and asked more questions than it answered, but they felt pleased with their afternoon's work. And they were especially pleased that they had been able to get their vision to this level without being interrupted.

1. Pick an idea.

Think about a particular idea that you'd like to share with business colleagues. The idea could be most anything, from an insight you gleaned from a financial spreadsheet to a brilliant blog you read online to a new marketing message you'd like to propose. Since you'll be thinking about this idea for a while, pick something that you find personally interesting and which is relatively easy to explain.

If you're stumped, here are a few examples:

- A new ad for our product, based on a princess kissing a frog.
- We don't calculate profitability correctly.
- In the past year, China became the world's second largest auto manufacturer behind the United States.

2. Draw a circle and give it a name.

Get a stack of six sheets of blank letter-size paper and a black pen. On the first sheet, draw a circle in the center of the page.

Now give your idea a name. It could be as descriptive as "a plan for redefining how we calculate profit and loss," as abstract as "the frog campaign," or as simple as

"China: 10 million cars and counting." Don't spend too much time on selecting the name—for now you're going to be the only person who will even hear it—but pick something that has meaning for you and your idea.

Write your idea's name in the center of the circle and write the SQVID letters below it.

3. Create your SQVID pages.

On each of the five remaining pages, write the word that corresponds to the SQVID letter at the upper left, and the opposite word on the lower left. When you are finished, you should have five sheets with one set of two words written on each.

- Simple-Elaborate

- Qualitative-Quantitative

- Vision-Execution

- Individual-Comparison

- Change-Status quo

They will look like this:

4. Fill out Your SQVID.

On each of the five sheets, make a quick sketch of how you might visually represent your idea according to each word. For example, if we had picked "the frog campaign," we might have something like this:

Complete a simple set of sketches for each sheet. If you need inspiration, go back and review your apples at the beginning of this chapter.

What Is Happening

The act of filling out the SQVID forces your mind's eye to look at your idea from many sides in a structured and repeatable way. The five questions you've just answered make different demands upon how your mind *sees* and activate many different thought centers in your brain, from those that notice measurement and shape to those that register time, space, and change. The sketches you've drawn visually represent all the fundamental ways you can see an idea. The exercise not only stretches the imagination, it simultaneously brings your idea into clearer focus, ready to be finalized for showing in the next chapters.

CHAPTER 7

FRAMEWORKS FOR SHOWING

Way back when we started talking about the visual thinking process, I mentioned that many people are uncertain about how to solve problems with pictures because they are uncertain about their ability to draw. This tendency to equate visual thinking with the creation of elaborate and refined drawings is just plain wrong. It approaches the process of visual thinking backward, limiting our most powerful problem-solving ability before we've even had a chance to really use it.

That's because *showing*—the step that contains the closest thing to a drawing lesson—happens at the end of the visual thinking process, not the beginning. In fact, businesspeople who try to start the process with showing—which is what happens 90 percent of the time—get so distracted by drawing skills, computer programs, and visual polish that they miss the real value of this step. *Showing* is not only our chance to wrap up our ideas so that we can share them with somebody else, this step is also when we invariably make our biggest breakthroughs—*but only if we've already looked, seen, and imagined well.*

Where the Rubber Meets the Road

Showing is where it all comes together. We looked, we saw, we imagined; we found patterns, made sense of them, and found ways to visually manipulate them into a picture never before seen. Showing is how we share this picture with others, both to inform and persuade them—and to check for ourselves whether others see the same things.

In order to *show* well, we need to complete three steps: Select the right framework, use that framework to create our picture, and then explain our picture to somebody else. Only one of those steps requires any drawing, and yet that's the one that nearly everybody gets hung up on.

The Three Steps of Showing

1. Select the right framework.

To get started, we need two tools to select the right framework. We've already used the SQVID to help focus our idea, and now we'll use it again, along with a new tool that we'll see in a moment, to select the best framework for composing our picture. It won't be difficult because there are only six frameworks to choose from—and again, we've already seen them all.

2. Use the framework to create our picture.

With the most appropriate framework selected for the problem we need to solve, we'll start by laying in the appropriate coordinate system, then gradually adding in the data and visual details that make our picture show (and tell) the right story.

3. Present and explain our picture.

Whether we'll be there in person to present it or not, our picture still needs an explanation. Sometimes that may take a thousand words, sometimes none at all. Either way, a good problem-solving picture is always straightforward to explain, no matter how complex its content or meaning. If the picture has been drawn according to the six ways we see and takes advantage of precognitive attributes, our audience will almost always "get" it long before we've stopped explaining.

Seeing Becomes Showing

> *Showing Step 1. Select the Right Framework.*

Chapter 5 closed with the idea that being aware of how we see isn't just useful in helping us break problems down into distinct visual elements, but also provides guidance on how we can *show*. Here's what that really means: Since our vision system normally sees things according to specific pathways, it makes sense to take advantage of those same pathways when creating pictures that other people are going to see. In other words, if we *see* in six ways, it makes sense that we should be able to *show* in six ways as well.

This is important—in many ways this is the key not only to the rest of this chapter, but to all visual thinking. To make this connection clearly visible, let's start with a quick review of the six ways we see.

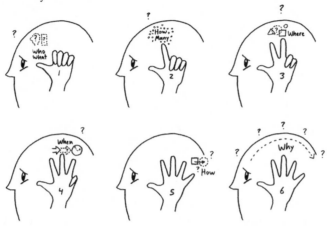

The six ways we see (again): *who/what, how many, where, when, how, and why.*

As we continue, let's keep our eyes wide open. The next step leads to the biggest and most useful insight in this book—the <6><6> rule of visual thinking.

The

<6><6>

Rule

For every one of the six ways of seeing, there is one corresponding way of showing.

For each one of these six ways of showing, there is a single visual framework that serves as a starting point.

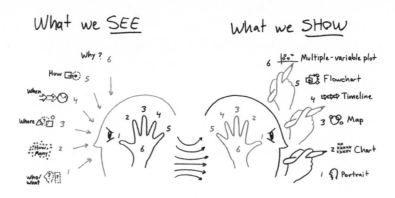

Walking through the picture from left to right, we see the six ways of seeing coming in through our eyes, being processed in our mind's eye, then flipping around and emerging as six corresponding *showing* pictures on the other side: *Who/what* becomes a **portrait,** *how many* becomes a **chart,** *where* becomes a **map,** *when* becomes a **timeline,** *how* becomes a **flowchart,** and *why* becomes a **multiple-variable plot.**

Since everything in the rest of the book relies on this concept, let's make sure we really get it. Here's the way it looks from our own eyes, a kind of "inside-looking-out" view of the same idea.

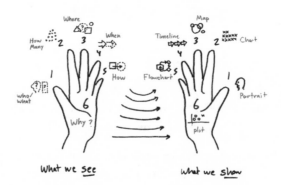

Of course, it's not really our hands that pass off the visual inputs to the corresponding outputs, but since we're going to need our hands to create upcoming pictures, now is a good time to draw them in. Also, using our hands to model the rule (especially since we've conveniently got the right number of fingers and palms) makes it easy to visualize and hard to forget.

IMPLICATIONS FOR VISUAL THINKING

The <6><6> model has many implications for visual thinking, all of them good:

- There may be thousands of possible charts we can make, but all are derived from just six basic "showing frameworks" (or a combination of those six).

- Learning when to apply these six frameworks and how to draw them gives us the ability to create a pictorial representation of almost any problem we can see.

The inverse is also true:

- Any problem that we can *see* (and that we can break down into its 6 W's fundamentals), can also be *shown* by simply representing those same 6 W's.

- The most efficient way to show a particular visual category (*who/what, how much, etc.*) is to just flip around the way we see it in the real world. If we see *where* based on objects' spatial relationships to each other, we can represent it by drawing those objects in a similar spatial position. If we see *when* by noting an object's change over time, we can represent it by drawing the same object as it appears at different times.

This means that we can forget about the hundreds of different kinds of charts, graphs, diagrams, pictograms, schematics, plots, maps, renderings, illustrations, and visualizations we run across in business. Not that there's anything wrong with having such a vast quantity of pictures available—on the contrary, they're all useful in the right context (and we'll soon see many of them in play)—but as we move into understanding the *showing* process, we need to worry about only six fundamental frameworks, not a thousand.

So the next time we face a problem, we won't have to ask ourselves, "Oh, boy, which picture could I possibly use to solve this problem?" We'll simply ask, "Which of the six frameworks maps to the problem I see?"

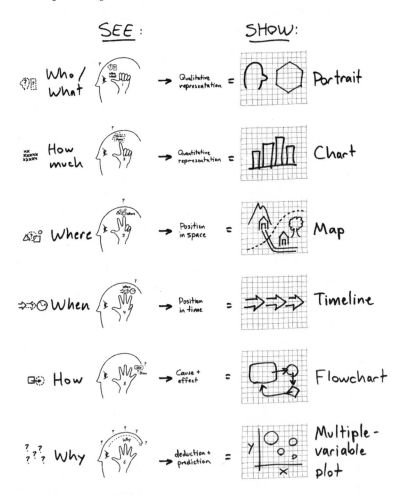

The six ways we *see* and the six ways we *show*.

What Defines a Showing Framework?

In order for these frameworks to be useful—both as starting points for visually thinking through ideas and as tools for drawing actual pictures—they must be comprehensive as a group (so that we can rely on just the six for most every picture we'll need to make) and yet individually distinct enough so that we know when to call upon each. To help us, there are four criteria that we will use to define each framework and differentiate them from one another.

1. **What the framework shows.** *Who/what, how much, where, when, how,* or *why,* as determined by cross-referencing what we saw with the <6><6> model.

2. **The framework's underlying coordinate system.** The fundamental structure of the picture, whether spatial, temporal, conceptual, or causal. This is also derived from the <6><6> model.

3. **The relationship between the objects contained within the framework.** Objects defined by their own traits, objects defined by their quantity, objects defined by their positions in space, objects defined by their positions in time, objects defined by their influences upon one another, objects defined by interactions of two or more of the above.

4. **The framework's starting point.** Top, center, beginning, end, etc.

As we go through each framework over the following pages, we'll continually refer back to these four criteria as a way to keep the frameworks distinct in our minds and to help us as we begin to draw examples of each one.

HOW DO WE USE A SHOWING FRAMEWORK?

The showing frameworks help us in three profound ways. First, they show us that creating meaningful problem-solving pictures isn't a random or chance event. On the contrary, the frameworks show that there is a logical reason for picking one type of picture over another, and that the process is learnable and repeatable. Second, the act of simply selecting one of the frameworks forces us to think through what it is that we *see* that is most important to *show*. If it's the people who matter most—the *who*—then we'll use a portrait. If it's the timing that matters most—the *when*—then we'll use a timeline, and so on. Finally, by providing us with a defined coordinate system and specific starting point, each framework gives us the way to get our picture started without confusion or worry.

VISUAL THINKING FRAMEWORKS: A SUMMARY OF TRAITS AND DIFFERENCES

Framework type	What it shows	Coordinate system	Objects' relationship	Starting point	Example
1. Portrait	Who/what	Inferred (usually spatial)	Defined by object's own physical traits	Object name	Typical customer
2. Chart	How much	amount, B, A, object(s)	Objects' relative quantities	Coordinate A name	Product sales sales, A B C D product

3. Map	*Where*		Objects' positions in space		
4. Timeline	*When*		Objects' positions in time		
5. Flowchart	*How*		Objects' influences upon each other		
6. Multiple-variable plot	*Why*		Objects' interactions involving any two or more of the above		

Mapping It All Together: The Visual Thinking Codex

Now we've got two different ways to think about showing our problem: the six frameworks derived from the <6><6> model, and the five imagination-focusing questions of the SQVID. These two models look different, function differently, and even force our minds to think in different ways: more analytically when we go about selecting a framework, and more intuitively when we run an idea through the SQVID. These differences are important because they make the two models complementary. It's when we use them together that solutions literally begin to appear on the page.

Imagine that we're running a major project and we've got to explain to our team leaders when a series of individual milestones must be completed to ensure on-time delivery. Timing is the critical factor here (*when*) so the <6><6> model tells us that the right framework for showing this information is a timeline. That's a good starting point, but knowing that we need to create a timeline doesn't tell us how detailed it needs to be, whether it should show steps as approximate durations or minute-by-minute deadlines, whether it compares typical project timing against the urgency required this time, etc.

In other words, we still need to determine which version of timeline to create, given the specific circumstances and audience we face: a simple timeline or an elaborate one, a qualitative version or a quantitative version, one that focuses on the vision of where we're going or the execution of how we're going to get there, one that shows this project alone or one that compares it to other simultaneous projects, a timeline that reflects the way things could be or simply the way things are. That's where the SQVID comes in. Because the SQVID forces us to answer each of these questions up front, it serves to focus our thinking and help us make important choices about our picture before we put pen to paper.

When we map the <6><6> and the SQVID together on a shared grid, a master list emerges that illustrates and categorizes every major problem-solving picture we'll use for the rest of this book. This list is called the Visual Thinking Codex, and using it is simple. At the intersection of each framework and each point of the SQVID are two icons, one for each SQVID option (simple vs. elaborate, quality vs. quantity, etc.). These icons represent the ideal starting point for any picture, taking into account what is most important to emphasize, depending on our audience, communications priorities, data, and personal viewpoint.

To use the codex, we first select the appropriate framework on the vertical axis

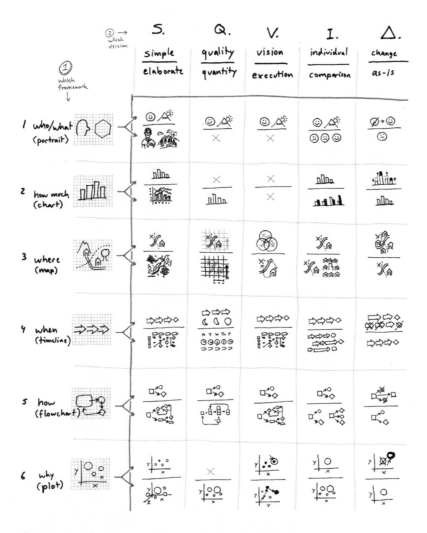

The Visual Thinking Codex: a master list of problem-solving pictures.

(portrait for *who,* map for *where,* etc.), then slide across the horizontal axis using the points of the SQVID to select the best version of that framework. In some cases, no icon appears because no appropriate version of that framework exists (there is no reason to qualitatively show *how much,* for example.)

Let's now run through that previous project management example using the codex.

Step 1. Showing when things need to get done in order to meet a final deadline is primarily a *when* problem, so we slide down the codex to the *when* row. Clearly, we're going to be making a timeline.

Step 2. Given the detailed and precise information we need to convey to our team leaders, we see as we slide across the SQVID that our timeline is going to be elaborate, quantitative, and execution oriented—a kind of super timeline showing the specific interaction of many precise deadlines of many project components. That's where we're going to start.

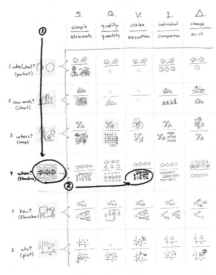

To test the codex again, let's now imagine that we're Daphne, the brand manager for the global publishing company from way back in chapter 1. We plan to go to our CEO to get his or her support for the new branding project we want to start. Getting support from the CEO is almost always a question of *why*—Why is this important to our growth? Why does it need to happen now? Why will Wall Street like it?—so this is a very different problem than the previous one, and it requires a completely different kind of picture.

Step 1. We slide down the axis to the *why* row: We'll be making a multiple-variable plot. Ouch. Those are the hardest of all pictures to create well and to show well. Then again, nobody said getting support from the CEO was easy. This will require some homework.

Step 2. We can make it an easier sell if we can show how our project aligns directly with the CEO's vision of the company, so let's make this a visionary plot.

Step 3. It will be even more persuasive if our picture shows how our project can help our company shift market position upward relative to our competitors—something the CEO's been talking about for years. To show that kind of picture, the codex tells us we should start with a *visionary, comparative, multiple-variable plot*—tricky, but worth the effort if it succeeds in showing the full story.

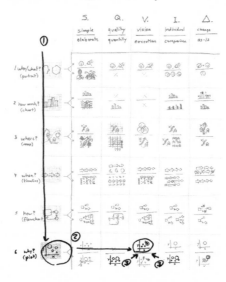

In both cases, whether we're managing a major project and need a detailed timeline or we're Daphne in search of the right plot, we've got our starting framework and version selected. In the first case, we're going to start with a super-timeline; for Daphne, it will be a visionary, comparative, multiple-variable plot. The codex has done it's job, now it's up to us to start drawing.

A NOTE ON COMBINATION FRAMEWORKS

The beauty of the <6><6> model is that by presenting a simple way of looking at the endless variety of possible pictures out there (and mapping them according to the six basic ways we see), it makes it easy to select the right starting point for showing almost anything we want to . . . almost.

The fact is that *how* and *why* aren't the only combinations we see. The miracle of our vision system is that it continuously combines *all* the ways we see in order to help us understand our environment. We see *when* in combination with *where*, we see *how much* in combination with *what*, etc. Two combinations—hybrid frameworks that are created by combining two of the basic six—are so frequently used in *showing* that we're going to identify them specifically as we run through each of the basic frameworks in the coming pages.

The first is the time series chart, the combination that results when a *how much* chart is superimposed on a *when* timeline. We'll discuss this combination in the *when* framework section in chapter 13. The second is the value chain, the result of combining a *when* timeline with a *how* flowchart, which we'll encounter in the *how* framework section in chapter 14.

Two combination frameworks appear often enough in problem-solving pictures that we're going to look at them in detail over the coming pages.

PART III
DEVELOPING IDEAS

The Visual Thinking MBA:
Putting Visual Thinking to Work

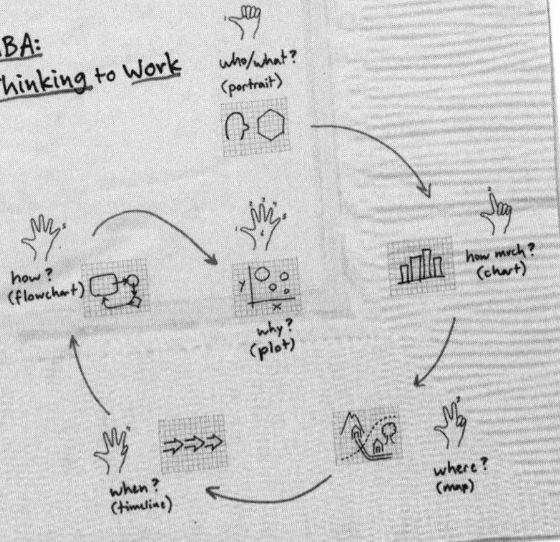

who/what?
(portrait)

how much?
(chart)

how?
(flowchart)

why?
(plot)

when?
(timeline)

where?
(map)

CHAPTER 8

SHOWING AND THE VISUAL THINKING MBA

Ladies and Gentlemen, Start Your Pens

After we've identified our problem, selected the appropriate showing framework, and further focused our ideas using the SQVID, the next step is to put pen to paper (or napkin or whiteboard) and start drawing. There are two ways we can look at what we're about to do. If we're a Black Pen person, it's going to be the easiest thing in the world; if we're a Red Pen person, it's going to be impossible, and there's no way we'll produce anything worth showing anybody. Both views are wrong. Drawing our picture is going to be harder than expected for the artistically gifted among us (because we'll be forcing our brains into potentially unfamiliar analytic processes); and it's going to be easier than expected for the "I'm not visual" crowd (because we'll be taking unexpected advantage of analytic capabilities we use all the time). The important thing to keep in mind at this point is that we already know what to do. We *looked* well, we *saw* clearly, we *imagined* confidently—we've even got our starting framework selected.

Here's how this is going to work: Since each framework requires a different way of approaching a drawing, we're going to run through an example or two of each. That is plenty enough to cover everything we've talked about in the book so far, but nowhere near enough to cover every problem we might face in the world. But that's the real beauty of visual thinking. It doesn't take many pictures to see how just a few frameworks and rules make any problem easy to picture.

The Visual Thinking MBA: Putting It All to Work

In business school, MBA students and executives rely on case studies to put into practice the theories of finance, operations, marketing, and management that they've learned in the classroom. Whether based on actual companies facing historically accurate business challenges or hypothetical situations featuring fictional businesses, the case studies are the backbone of MBA programs because they make abstract ideas "real." In part III, we're going to take the same approach. By walking through a detailed case study, we're going to make the tools and rules of visual thinking come alive.

Using a fictitious software company in crisis as a backdrop, we're going to put everything we've discussed into play: the visual thinking process, the SQVID, the <6><6> model, and the codex. To really show how effective visual thinking can be in understanding a complex business problem, we're going to use these tools to create pictures covering everything we would see in a business school seminar. Starting with customer research, we'll then move through marketing and product development, financial analysis, project planning, and finally strategic decision making. In short, there's going to be a lot to look at.

As with any rigorous case study, there are two ways to approach this: either as a top-level scan or as a detailed deep dive. To help readers who want to make a quick scan, this case study is broken into six chapters, one showcasing each of the six visual frameworks. If you're mainly interested in the frameworks themselves, read just the first two or three summary pages of each chapter—you'll still get a great sense of the overall business story.

If you're interested in following the entire line of reasoning in detail, start from the beginning. As you work your way through, you'll notice that each picture is created step by step over a series of frames—almost like a stop-action animation—to help you see exactly how each is composed. Either way—scan or deep dive—this is where solving business problems with pictures becomes real.

The Case Study Scenario

Imagine that we work for an accounting software company called Super Accounting Exchange Incorporated, or SAX Inc. SAX has been designing and selling specialized accounting software for use by large organizations since 1996, and although SAX isn't a very big company, our flagship product has been an industry benchmark for nearly a decade.

In our niche industry there are presently five main competitors, all with their own approaches to the business and all with their own strengths and weaknesses. The five are:

- SAX Inc. *(That's us)*
- SMSoft Inc.
- Peridocs Incorporated
- Univerce LLC
- MoneyFree

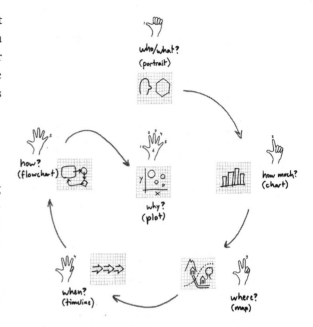

Starting with a basic *who* problem at SAX Inc., we're going to run through all six frameworks, creating several pictures that take us from defining the problem to arriving at a solution.

So here's the problem: For the past two years our sales have gone flat while sales at the other companies have continued to rise. Our latest product release a year ago introduced many new features, making our software the most feature-rich available, but our customers' reception has been lukewarm. Our sales reps complain that they're having an increasingly hard time selling our expensive software, given the rise of "open-source freeware" over the past year. Such freeware—typically created by loosely affiliated developers unencumbered by the overhead costs and shareholder demands seen in a bigger business like ours—is making increasing inroads into the technology industry everywhere. So far no open-source freeware comes close to our feature set, but that won't last forever. We don't know exactly what we need to do before we lose significant market share, but we know we have to do something. So let's move on to chapter 9 and start at the beginning, with our customers.

A NOTE ON THE PICTURES
WE'LL BE CREATING

Before we get started, it's worth revisiting an earlier comment about the images in this book. Everything we're about to create is intended to be drawn by hand: on a whiteboard, on a yellow pad, on the back of a napkin, on whatever drawing surface you might have in front of you. In the introduction I said that Daphne's strategy chart was the first and last picture in the book to be created on a computer, and that remains true. While computers are insanely wonderful tools for countless applications, I can't think of anything that they add to visual thinking at this level—while I can think of several things they take away. In fact, because using a computer seems to mask a number of our basic cognitive tasks—especially the unexpected ideas that emerge when we put pen to paper—relying on computers at this stage is more likely to undermine our visual thinking abilities than to advance them.

On the plus side, it's also true that computers make the composition and finishing of the more advanced pictures infinitely easier than anything we can do by hand, are essential for creating accurate quantitative images, and are irreplaceable presentation and communication tools. Those points are all not trivial. That's why appendix B is included: It addresses which software I find most useful for further developing each framework, and introduces a few simple software tricks that will be helpful if you decide to go the entirely digital (and I don't mean fingers) route.

But for now, let's stay with pens and napkins: It's good practice for the next time we meet someone interesting at an airport bar.

CHAPTER 9

WHO ARE OUR CUSTOMERS?

PICTURES THAT SOLVE A *WHO/WHAT* PROBLEM

> **Framework 1: To show a who/what problem, use a portrait.**

The Customer Crisis

e all agree: We don't know our customers as well as we should anymore, and in order to figure out which customers to go out and talk to, we need to create a portrait of who we think they are. Let's pick a large client company and use what we know about it to create a sample baseline customer profile. We know that our baseline will contain a lot of information, that we'll want to be able to look at it from many different angles, and that we'll share it inside and outside our company, so it makes sense to create a picture.

We already know how to pick the right framework: Look it up on the Visual Thinking Codex. In this case our problem is about people (*who* our customers are), so the codex tells us to start with a portrait, or *qualitative representation*.

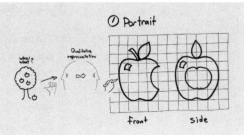

Framework type	What it shows	Coordinate system	Objects' relationship	Starting point	Example
1. Portrait	Who/what	Inferred (usually spatial)	Defined by an object's own physical traits	Object name	Typical customer

Recall that the first way of seeing was *who* and *what*, meaning that we saw objects that we recognized because of distinct visual qualities: their components, shape, proportion, size, color, texture, etc. To show to others what we saw, we create a portrait (or *qualitative* representation) that represents the most evident of those qualities, emphasizing especially those that made our object visually distinct from others. While portraits don't show *how many* of something there are, *where* they are, or *when* and *how* they interact—all of which are addressed by the other specific frameworks—they do provide the starting point by helping us identify and keep track of *who is who* and *what is what*.

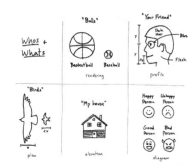

Renderings, profiles, plans, elevations, diagrams: There are lots of kinds of portraits, but all show the same things—the recognizable qualities that differentiate objects.

Our products are:

Worth
their weight
in gold

⛤ Stellar

💮 Best in class

⚖ On par

🖥 Out of date

☺ Lousy

Worth
improving

Worth
checking

👤 Unpopular

🏛 Unsold

Creating even the simplest of portraits engages the mind's eye.

Our customers are:

Here to
stay

😆 Ecstatic

☺ Pleased

😊 In cahoots

😐 Satisfied

😕 So-so

😑 Ambivalent

• Distant

😠 Angry

✦ Nonexistent

already
gone

Even the sparest of portraits make comparisons come alive.

Portraits: General Rules of Thumb

1. **Think simple.** The goal isn't to be Rembrandt. In fact, an overly elaborate or cute picture inevitably draws too much attention to itself and distracts from the essence of the idea to be conveyed. The simpler, the better: Think visually telegraphing an idea 😊 rather than painting the whole picture .

2. **Illuminate lists.** The purpose of creating a business portrait is to trigger the unexpected qualitative ideas that emerge when the hands and the mind's eye work together. Visually representing someone or something (regardless of actual likeness or detail) always triggers insights that writing a list alone cannot achieve.

3. **Visually describe.** When time is limited (and in business, time is always limited), pictures always make for better comparisons than verbal descriptions. Comparative portraits can be as simple as a series of smiley faces. Adding even that thin a visual aspect brings objects to life and makes them memorable.

With these ideas in mind, let's go back to our customer portrait. With our framework selected, we then look across the SQVID, answering its five questions as we go.

② → which version	S. simple elaborate	Q. quality quantity	V. vision execution	I. individual comparison	△. change as is
① which framework ↓					
I who/what (portrait)	☺ / ▲ ✗	☺ / ▲ ✗	☺ / ▲ ✗	☺ / ▲ ☹ ☺ ☺	∅ → ☺ ☹

Simple or *elaborate?* Given that this is our first effort at visually portraying our customers, we'd be better off with something simple. *Qualitative* or *quantitative?* For now, this is just a portrait, not a numeric representation, so by default it will be qualitative. *Vision* or *execution?* As a baseline, we're not yet talking about where we'd like to go or how to get there, so that question doesn't matter for this picture; let's skip it. *Individual* or *comparison?* Since we'll be looking across the whole range of customers, this will be a comparison. *Change* or *as is?* Since we're hoping to see the baseline, our picture will be as is for now, although depending on what we find, we may want to show *change* at some point. Summing up, this is a pretty simple starting framework—*a simple, qualitative portrait of a few customer types,* something like this: ☹ ☺ ☺ Now we're finally ready to draw.

What to start with? Before thinking too hard, it's helpful to know that although the first mark on the napkin is the most difficult to make, it is also among the least important. We'll be adding to it, altering it, and possibly erasing it entirely. It's more important that we get *something* down on paper than worry too much about what it is. A good way to start *any* picture is to draw a circle and give it a name. Since we've already agreed that we don't know our customers as well as we should, let's start with something we do know—*us.*

Let's start with a simple circle and then give it a name.

Since a portrait is intended to help us identify one object from another, let's add something visual to make "us" more distinctly *us*—our building, for example.

Remember this is a portrait, so let's add our building to make us more recognizable.

Does seeing ourselves portrayed this way trigger any ideas about how to show our sample client? How about we add them in the same way?

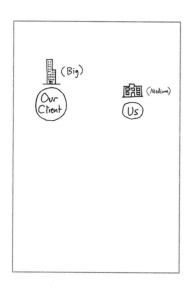

We add in our client and already we've got a good picture going.

Even this spare picture starts to show us something about the relationship between us and our client, and helps our mind's eye begin imagining ways to create a portrait of our customers.

So if we're going to be showing people, why don't we again start with our own? That won't tell us anything about our customers, but drawing *us* (who we know so well) will get us in the right frame of mind for thinking about *them*.

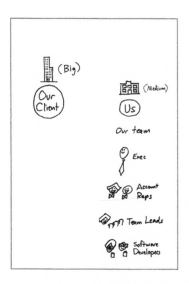

We draw in the people of our own company: the boss, the account reps, team leads, and developers.

That's us. All those smiley faces we talked about are starting to appear. Loosened up by drawing ourselves in, we're finally ready to sketch in our customers.

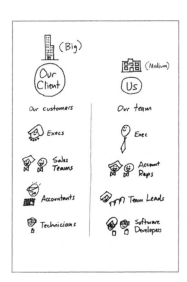

We draw in the customers that our people sell to: our client's execs, sales teams, accountants, and technical folks.

There they are: our customers. Interesting. There are more types than we might have initially thought. Just creating a portrait like this has already started us thinking about customers in different ways. So far we've spent just a couple minutes with this picture, yet we've already created a baseline portrait of who's who in our business and have triggered many new ideas simply because we drew it. There's only one more thing we've got to do before we start making copies: Label everything.

We've instinctively been giving names to the shapes as we've drawn them in. In fact, right from the beginning our task was to give a name to our first circle. As we added more people we kept labeling them, too. For good reason: While our brain's visual centers are happy to have pictures to look at, other mental processing areas demand names, and if they're not written there, we're going to make the names up ourselves. It's always better to be proactive about labeling and leave no doubt about what we're showing.

We also always need to give our pictures a title. While it should be completely clear to us what we just drew, it always pays to assume that someone else is going to approach our picture from a different perspective, perhaps completely missing the point we intended to make. So as a rule, spell it out right on the top, every time.

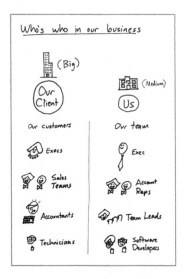

By adding a title we know that we're being clear about what we're showing to anyone who sees our picture.

Simple as it is, this picture is useful as a backbone for mapping in other qualitative traits about our customers. We know from previous market studies, for example, that each of these customer types wants something different from accounting software. Client executives are ultimately responsible for anything good (or bad) that happens whenever our software gets used, so they want a product that is easily accessible to their own people and impenetrable to anyone else. Above all, execs want *security*. Sales teams want a product that makes it easy for them to sell their company's services, so they want software with a good reputation—they want a *salable* brand. Accountants want accuracy and stability; they want *reliability*. And technicians want software that is easy to connect to other systems and easy to update, they want *flexibility*. That's a long list of wants, just the kind of thing more easily digested in a picture.

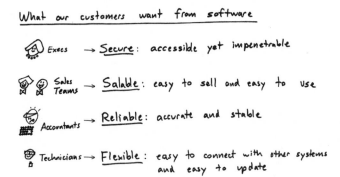

Adding what they want.

Now we have two portraits of our customers, one showing who they are, and another showing what they want. These are just two of many versions we can make. In different businesses and different contexts, similar pictures might be called renderings, plans, diagrams, or elevations, but all do essentially the same thing: They provide a visual record of what something looks like, the *who* and *what* that we see.

CHAPTER 10

HOW MANY ARE BUYING?

PICTURES THAT SOLVE A *HOW MUCH* PROBLEM

> **Framework 2: To show a how much *problem*, use a chart.**

The Customer Crisis, Now with Numbers

We've seen our customers, noted some of their distinctions, and even begun thinking about what they might want from our company's software. That's good information that will be useful for helping us get sales moving again, but it's only a start. To be meaningful, we're going to need to know *how many* of each of those customers we have, quantify *how much* they're willing to spend on products like ours, and even try to numerically measure how they feel about us and our products.

We're not talking about *who* and *what* anymore. Now we need to see *how much*. The Visual Thinking Codex tells us that we're going to shift to charts now—pictures that show quantities, illustrate measurable criteria, and represent numeric comparisons.

Unlike portraits, which we could create without any specific quantitative information, charts demand numbers, measures, and data.

REVIEW: A CHART SHOWS *HOW MUCH*

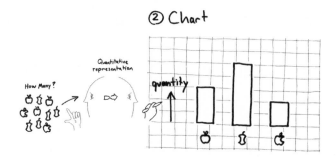

Framework type	What it shows	Coordinate system	Objects' relationship	Starting point	Example
2. Chart	*How much*		Objects' relative quantities		

After *who* and *what*, we next saw *how much* or *how many* objects there were. For small-ish numbers, our minds did a quick count; for slightly larger quantities, we made rough estimates; for large quantities we just said to ourselves, "A lot." To show these numbers to others, we use a chart (or *quantitative representation*) in which we turn abstract numbers into visually concrete pictures of amounts.

Charts: General Rules of Thumb

1. **It's the data that matters, so let it show.**
Many people find numbers boring, so we jazz up our charts with visual bells and whistles hoping to make the pictures look more interesting. Three thoughts: First, insightful data is never boring. If what we're showing resonates with our audience (either because it shows exactly what they hoped for or surprises the daylights out of them), they won't fall asleep. Second, we should always show the fewest possible pictures to make our point. Either limit the number of one-point pictures we show or combine as many data points as possible into one or two multiple-variable plots (more on those later). And third, the addition of low-key anthropomorphic elements ☹ ☺ ☺ *where appropriate* does add cognitive engagement. In other words, if you're counting people, go ahead and show the people.

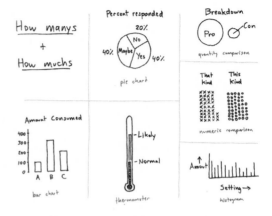

Pie charts, bar charts, numeric comparisons, histograms: There are countless ways of representing *how much*, but they are all variations on the same theme—providing a visual measurement of quantity.

2. **Pick the simplest model to make your point.** This year's version of the most popular spreadsheet software* includes ninety-nine different charting choices right out of the box. *No wonder we're confused about which chart to use.* The fact is, it only *looks* like it has ninety-nine. In actuality, it has four—bars, lines, pies, and bubbles. Everything else is a jazzed-up version of one of those. If we think of those four types like this, we shouldn't have any trouble picking the right one.

---

* If you're interested in a detailed explanation of when to use each of the myriad types of charts available, there are lots of great books out there. See Appendix B: Resources for Visual Thinkers for recommendations.

- Bars: For comparing absolute quantities of something (1,000 apples versus 800 oranges versus 120 pears).

- Lines and areas: For comparing absolute quantities between two different criteria or times (pies have 1,000 apples, 0 oranges, and 60 pears while tarts have 0 apples, 800 oranges, and 60 pears). (We'll look at times series charts in *when* frameworks, chapter 12.)

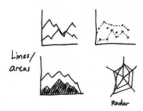

- Pies: For comparing relative quantities of something (52 percent apples, 42 percent oranges, and 6 percent pears).

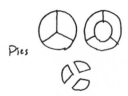

- Bubbles: For comparing more than two variables (which we'll look at when we come to *why* frameworks, chapter 14).

3. If you start with one model, stay with one model. If our chart has the right coordinate system to convey our data and is built with precognitive attributes, our audiences should get it in no time. Nevertheless, once they've "learned" to read our first chart, don't jar their "seeing settings" by suddenly flopping an axis, changing the chart type, or introducing a wildly divergent way of thinking. Think of showing a series of charts as a drive through a beautiful landscape: Gentle or expected transitions are pleasant; suddenly flying out over a cliff is not.

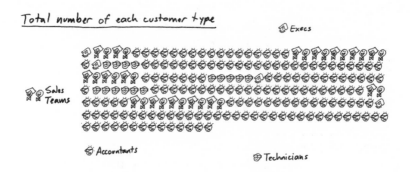

Our sales data tells us exactly how many customers we have.

Back to SAX Inc. While making our customer portrait, we collected the *who* data; now we need some *how many* numbers. As we look at our company's sales records, it turns out that we have those numbers after all. Since "job title" is one of the fields in our software registration questionnaire, we have a record of how many customers of each type we have. If we were to create a picture showing both customers and quantities, it might look something like this.

Numerically speaking, this picture couldn't be any more accurate: It's as if we had all our customers stand in their parking lot and took a photo. But accuracy aside, there are major problems here: First, although we can pick out individual types, we can't see the groups (since they're all mixed together). Second, it's almost impossible to count. We can see quantity, but we can't be precise or do any math with it. So let's straighten out the coordinates and add summary numbers.

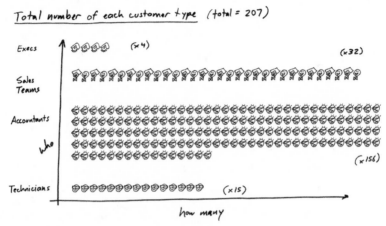

Total number of each customer type *(total = 207)*

Same image, now with numbers and coordinates added.

Much better. Shown this way, we can rank and compare each customer type instantly. We immediately see that there are a lot more accountants than salespeople, about half as many technicians as salespeople, and only a few execs. Still, it's a hard picture to draw. What we really need is a simpler way of showing those quantities without having to draw every one of the people. Let's try something: How about we get rid of the picture altogether and just show the numbers?

That also gives us numeric accuracy, but loses all the pictorial immediacy—it now takes our mind a few seconds to dance back and forth between the rows and columns in order to see how the customer numbers compare. A table also doesn't provide any hooks to catch our visual memory. If we

Total number of each customer type

who		how many
	execs	4
	sales	32
	accountants	156
	technicians	15

We could get rid of the picture altogether and substitute a table.

can't remember the precise numbers, we've got no larger context to fall back upon. What we need is a hybrid, something that combines the best of both pictures. What about a bar chart?

There we go. Easy to see *who* we're talking about and *how many* of each, plus we've got the numbers right there—we've even got precognitive quantity bars for our eyes to read immediately, compare, and viscer-

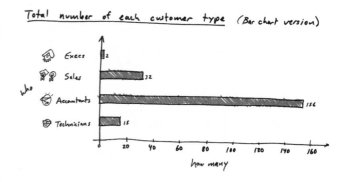

Total number of each customer type (Bar chart version)

A bar chart helps us see the pictures *and* the numbers.

ally recall long after we've forgotten the numbers: "I don't remember exactly how many, but I know there were a lot more accountants than salespeople." Perfect. If we need to see precisely how many in *total* there are of something, a simple bar chart is the way to go.

Seeing exactly how many customers we have is only part of the equation. What we really need to know is how many execs we sell to relative to accountants relative to salespeople. That's how we'll figure out who is most important to focus on given our fixed marketing budgets. If we've got only one pie's worth of marketing budget available, for example, we need to know who should get the biggest slice.

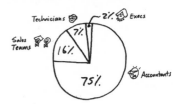

Total number of each customer type

Same thing as % of total, pie style

We use a pie chart to show quantities relative to the whole.

That's why we use a pie chart when we need to see percentages relative to the whole.

We don't see the total numbers anymore; instead we see how many of one customer type we have relative to others. If all customers were equally likely to buy our software, we'd want to divide up our marketing budget according to these same percentages. That way we'd know we were spreading out our marketing dollars evenly among all customers.

The great pie chart fight

There's a problem with pie charts: They're in the middle of a war.

VS

The battling parties.

Among information designers, there is a long-running battle raging about the effectiveness of pie charts for conveying data. On the one hand are people who think pie charts are fine—easy to create (with the right software), visually pleasing, and easy to read. On the other front are people who believe that since our eyes are less well adapted to accurately measuring proportional size differences in slices than they are in straight verticals and horizontals (which is true), we shouldn't ever use pie charts.

In fact, there is a time and a place for both, and the proof is in the pizza. If you've ever been to a kindergartener's birthday party, you'll have seen that six-year-olds have no problem picking the biggest piece of the pie. If they can figure it out, so can we. So if you prefer round pizza, feel free to use a pie chart. If you prefer your pizza square, there is an equivalent chart to fall back on: the stacked percentage chart. It shows the same information, just lays it out in straight lines.

If the differences among slices are so critical yet so small as to be difficult to visually detect, you're better off going back to a nonpictorial table anyway.

Total number of each customer type

Same thing as % of total, bar style

	2%	Execs
	16%	Sales Teams
100%	75%	Accountants
	7%	Technicians

The stacked pizza, or vertical percentage chart.

But that's one of the challenges with the typical *how much* chart. Because it shows only quantity, it's easy to forget other critical differences that might exist between the items being measured. In other words, although the numbers we see in a quantitative comparison may be accurate, they can still mislead us. For example, if the pie chart above were the only measure I had of customer quantity, I'd in theory have no choice but to assume that I should allocate 75 percent of my marketing budget to my accountant customers, since they represent 75 percent of registered users. But that might not at all reflect sales reality.

As we continue to look through our sales numbers, let's say that we come across the actual client purchase orders (POs). These POs show the final amounts paid and by whom—not who registered the software, but who bought it. Using another bar chart (since we're looking at absolute numbers, not percentages), we see that accountant customers spent $100,000 with us last year, while salespeople spent only $5,000.

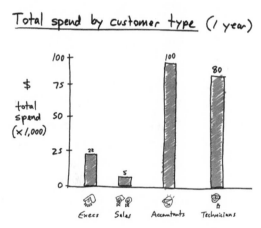

By total spend, accountants are our biggest customer group.

Here we see a different story emerge. While accountants represented three-quarters of our total registered customers, they bought only slightly more software than did the technicians, who were the second smallest customer group in size! That's interesting. Who'd have thought that the technical people were the ones doing so much buying?

To understand how this is true, we're going to have to look at one more chart. This time, let's factor in the quantity of each customer type against how much money each spent. Doing the math (total spend divided by number of customers per type) tells us the following: When we factor in the number of customers against their spending, we see that the average exec spends $5,500 on our software, the average tech $5,300, but the average accountant spends only $640.

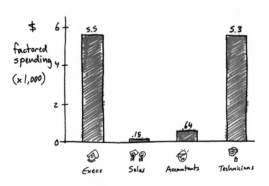

Factored spending per customer type (/ year)

By individual spending, execs and technicians are our biggest customers.

Whoa! Look at that. While execs and technicians account for just half of all purchases, individually each has nearly nine times the individual spending power of the accountants. Nothing we'd looked at in any data before would have led us to see that. Although this chart doesn't tell us *why* the numbers shake out like this, it certainly gives us a lot to think about. Perhaps the technicians are doing much of the buying on behalf of the accountants. If so, those technicians have tremendous spending power. And just four execs are buying even more? That tells us something new about purchase decision making at our client's: It falls disproportionately on the two most disparate groups. It also tells us that we'd better start looking carefully at the buying process of the technicians and execs.

All this should be giving us an inkling of where our sales problem may originate—and that's what we'll be looking at next: the *where* framework. But before we go there, let's review. The pictures shown here—numeric comparisons, pie charts, and bar charts—are just a few of the variety of ways to show *how much* or *how many*. As we saw with portraits, different businesses and different problems will demand different types of charts to represent quantity; but also like portraits, they are all just variations on the same theme. All are ways to show us *how many* or *how much* there are of the *whos* and *whats* we represented with our first framework.

Chapter 11

WHERE IS OUR BUSINESS?

PICTURES THAT SOLVE A *WHERE* PROBLEM

Framework 3: To show *a* **where** *problem, use a* **map.**

Moving Out Across the Map

The numbers we looked at in the previous chapter show that the executives and technicians at our client are doing a disproportionate amount of the buying. That was interesting and unexpected: We'd always assumed it was the accountants who bought most of our software since they were the ones who used it. This twist has got us wondering if we really understand the hierarchy of our client's business; it appears that the technicians are in a position of greater influence than we knew.

So now we've got a *where* problem—not a geographic "where" as in who is located in what building or which city—but rather a structural problem. We want to see *where* the now-critical technicians fit into the decision tree of our client's organization relative to its accountants, salespeople, and execs. What we need is a map of our client's business structure. And even though it's not really a geographic map, we go about creating it as if it were.

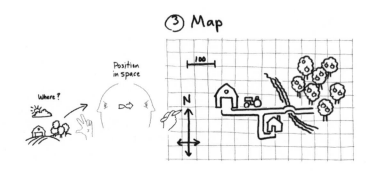

Framework type	What it shows	Coordinate system	Objects' relationship	Starting point	Example
3. Map	Where		Objects' positions in space		

After *how much*, we saw *where* objects were in relation to one another. We noted their positions, relative orientations, and distances apart. In order to show these locations to someone else, we use maps to represent placement, proximity, overlap, distance, and direction—and that doesn't apply just to geography: Maps make all kinds of ideas about the spatial relationships of objects unexpectedly clear.

Because of their versatility, maps are the most flexible of all six frameworks, which means that various kinds of maps may not look all that much alike. The fact is that they really are, especially in the way we go about making them and the spatial relationships they illustrate. If we start by drawing in the most prominent feature of our "landscape"—whether that is a mountain, a person, or an idea—and have a clear set of coordinates defined, it's a relatively straightforward matter to move outward and add more and more features and details, mapping overlays of complementary data on top to indicate everything from borders and distances to connections and sets of shared traits.

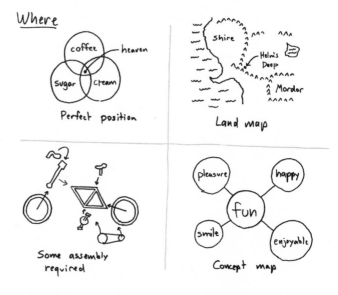

Maps can be Venn diagrams, schematics, landscapes, "think maps": No matter how different they may look, they're all drawn the same way and all show the same thing—the spatial relationship of one object to another.

Maps are the most familiar visual thinking framework we have: from organizational charts (which everybody knows how to draw) to Venn diagrams (which everybody understands) to good old treasure maps (which everybody loves to look at), maps are our most frequently used framework.

Maps: General Rules of Thumb

1. **Everything has a geography.** Anything that is built up from multiple unique components—whether those components are cities and rivers or concepts and ideas—can be mapped. The task for the visual thinker is to ask, "If these ideas (or nouns, concepts,

elements, components, etc.) were nations, where would their borders be—and what roads would connect them?"

2. **North is a state of mind.** We're used to thinking of maps with a north-south versus east-west coordinate system upon which places and objects are plotted according to their relative spatial positions. We can make maps of most anything using other pairs of opposites: good-bad versus expensive-cheap, high-low versus winners-losers. In fact, the only challenge with most maps is coming up with a meaningful coordinate system; once it's in place, plotting in the "landmarks" is easy.

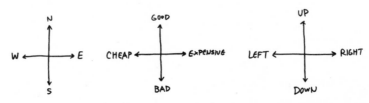

3. **Look beyond the obvious hierarchy.** Traditional (hierarchical) org charts are wonderful tools for mapping the official chain of command of an organization and for showing who is responsible for what. But when it comes to understanding where the less obvious—but usually more powerful—political connections really are, a bubble-based or connections-based "map of influence" is the better tool. The data to create such a map is always much harder to collect, but the effort pays off when insights into the inner workings of an organization are needed.

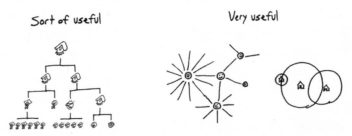

Once again, back to SAX Inc.: We know from the codex that a *where* problem demands a map, and as we run across the SQVID we think *simple, qualitative, visionary, individual,* and *as is.* We see that we'll need to create a picture somewhere between a concept model and a treasure map showing the structure of the company. We also know that the best way to start a map is to draw in the most prominent feature, which in our client's case is their massive accounting department, the "factory" of their entire operation.

We start the map of our client's business structure with their most prominent feature: their huge accounting operation.

Even though that's where all those accountants sit, we now know that accounting is not the home of our new target buyers, so let's branch out from there and add in the other divisions.

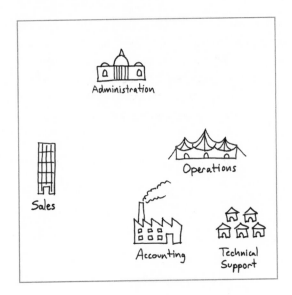

The main accounting factory is surrounded by administration, sales, and support divisions.

We also know that all those groups are run like little fiefdoms, so let's add in the borders to see who butts up against whom—and who doesn't share any borders at all.

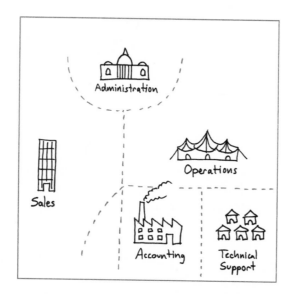

Adding borders shows us that sales is an independent state run by its own rules, while operations, accounting, and support share many common borders.

In the real world, adjacent nations are connected by roads, and the same is true with our client. Let's get one of our own salespeople—someone who knows how things really run over there in client land—to help us map in those interdepartmental pathways.

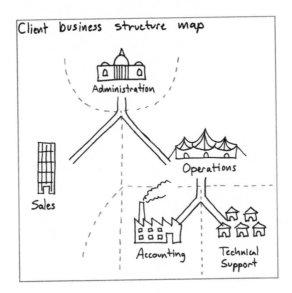

Client business structure map

Administration

Operations

Sales

Accounting

Technical Support

Based on the insights of our own salespeople into the client's organization, let's map in the roads between departments.

Hmm: No roads between sales and accounting. No direct connections means little influence one way or the other, so it's unlikely either is influencing the buying decisions of the other. OK, we've got our map. Now let's see where the treasure is.

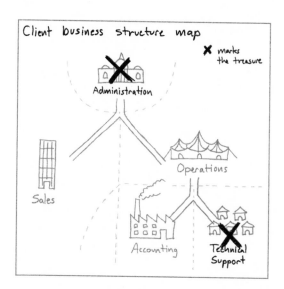

X's mark the spots where treasure (the people who buy our software) is buried.

We've now got a sense of the divisional structure of our client. That gives us a useful overview, but as we look at it, we realize that what we really need to see is the hierarchical connections between those domains: Who decides what and who influences whom. So let's make another map of the same "geography," but this time we'll focus on the real power—the people. We'll approach things in the same way, starting with the most prominent feature: in this case Marge, the CEO.

We start a map with the geography's most prominent feature, so begin with the CEO.

Since we'll be showing everybody else relative to Marge, we need to establish a coordinate system around her, some place to map in the next most prominent features: Mary (who runs sales) and Mildred (who runs operations).

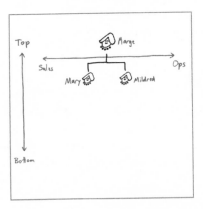

Two lines establish our coordinate system and allow us to start mapping in other people.

Pushing ahead, we next map in the middle management layer of Morgan, Tom, Dick, and Beth—the real gatekeepers of the business's domains. Then we decide to erase the coordinates after all, since they're complicating things and, let's face it, everybody knows which way is up on an org chart.

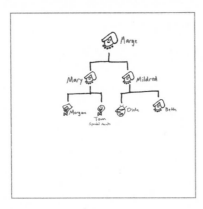

Middle management appears.

Then we map in the rank and file. Amazing. We've got most of the company mapped and we haven't even seen the technicians (half our buyers) yet.

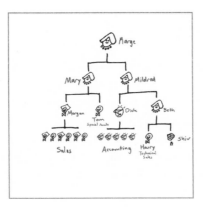

Four layers down and we still haven't seen the technicians.

One last layer and they finally appear, way at the bottom of the stack, far removed from Marge and the executives, and with no visible connections whatsoever back to the sales teams. Well, there we have it: Add a title and we're looking at the organizational map of our client, seeing the hierarchical location of each group in relation to the others.

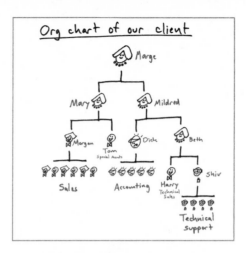

We're finished: a complete map of our client's hierarchical organization structure.

Org charts like this are one of the best examples of a *where* business map: Creating one illustrates how easy it is to show the spatial relationships of multiple items in a clear way, and—even better—org charts are the one kind of map that everybody in business (including, *especially including,* the "I'm not visual" people) knows how to draw with conviction. In fact, if anybody asked us to sketch out how our own company works, the first (most likely only) picture we'd draw is a hierarchical, top-to-bottom org chart.

We've all seen org charts, we all understand them, and, whether we're happy with our own position on them or not, find it comforting to see ourselves and people we know concretely represented in such an unequivocal framework. Because org charts give us a sense of confidence in the order of the world, we take great stock in them as accurate reflections of people's organizational influence over one another. This is a belief which, while true enough to keep org charts the favorite business picture of all time, can also make them wildly misleading. In fact, often the most insightful thing about an org chart is what it doesn't show. But to see that, we have to go looking in a different way.

Here's what I mean. Looking back at our org chart, we're faced with an anomaly.

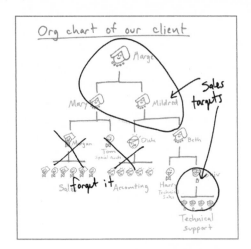

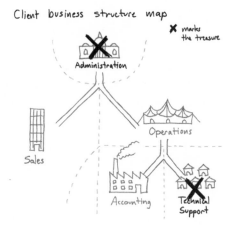

Neither map shows any direct connection between the execs and the techs—what's up?

According to our numbers, the execs and the technicians are the big buyers, but organizationally they are as far apart as two groups can get—and our first business structure map didn't show any direct "roads" linking them.

We *could* say that we've now got two distinct sales targets within the same client company who each require their own distinct marketing approach, but we'd much rather clarify the relationship between the two groups. By better understanding the connection, perhaps we could come up with a single, more cost-effective marketing approach that would appeal to both execs and technicians. That feels like a stretch, but it would certainly be worth the effort if we could find the common thread.

We're stumped until our own salesperson—the one who really knows how things work there—tells us the story of Jason, our client's technical whiz kid. It turns out

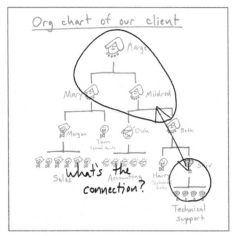

What's the critical connection between the execs and the techs?

that Jason, two years out of engineering school and in his first job with our client, is a genius at fixing laptops. He's already got such a great reputation that everybody calls him when they have a problem, and Jason has been able to solve so many problems for Mildred, the head of all operations, that she's come to rely on Jason's technical savvy for insights into everything technology related. So there's the connection: Jason. The lowest guy on the totem pole turns out to have the greatest technical exposure of anyone across the entire company.

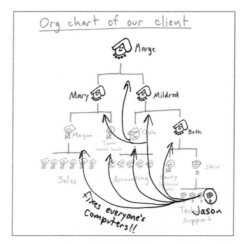

Aha! It turns out that Jason—the lowest guy on the whole totem pole—is the one everybody calls when their computer isn't working.

Now we've seen both the weakness and strength of a traditional org chart. Since it shows only the "official" structure, it doesn't illuminate many of the human connections that really make things work. Then again, once an org chart is mapped out, it becomes an excellent backbone for mapping in the real spheres of influence.

Size is one of the visual cues that we key off of without any hesitation. So if we were to create a set of overlays on top of the org chart we just created, we could use size as a way to quickly indicate the real influence of Jason within our client landscape. So let's take that same org chart and use different-size circles to indicate the relative technical influence of each person.

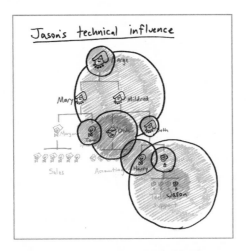

Jason's real importance becomes visible when we use different-size circles to indicate his technical influence over middle management and the execs.

We found the missing link: Jason. And if he has the ear of decision makers across the company, that makes him a powerful influence in technology-buying decisions. Whether or not he actually does the buying, he certainly is influencing it—both within the technology and accounting domains that account for most *total* purchases, as well as among the executives who make the greatest number of *individual* purchases. Given his influence, it makes sense to figure out what makes Jason say good things (or bad things) about a particular software package.

As a starting point, let's go back to the portrait we made showing what each of our customers looks for when choosing software, but this time try to map out the connections—perhaps we'll see what makes Jason tick. Starting from the top, we recall that executives want security.

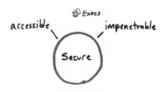

Execs value software security above all else.

Then we recall that accountants want reliability, which overlaps security slightly.

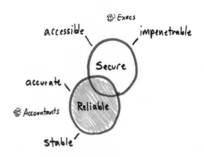

The reliability that accountants want shares some overlap with the execs.

Jason, trekking as he does through all levels of the company, knows that the best software doesn't just meet his own flexibility criteria (easy to connect to other systems and easy to update), it also meets the needs of the execs and accountants. And Jason knows their needs because he's the guy who has to listen every time something goes wrong. This means that the one person in the company who knows both what the software needs to do *and* has the reach to influence buying decisions across the company is the guy who barely even made the org chart.

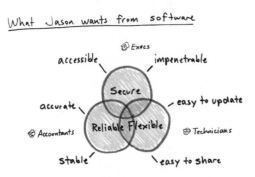

Jason's view of software intersects with that of both execs and accountants.

This map is called a Venn diagram and it is used to show the spatial overlap between any kind of objects, even ideas. Venn diagrams are a type of broader category of "concept maps" that don't look anything like either the treasure map or the org maps that we created, but do exactly the same thing: They show the same way of seeing (*where*), they share the same kind of coordinate system (spatial: up-down, right-left, front-back), are created the same way (start with the most prominent feature and add others in relative position around it), and represent the same thing—the relative positions of several objects *in space.*

Since the Venn diagram here does such a nice job of showing us what Jason looks for in accounting software, let's use a similar but more elaborate concept map to model out the basic components of *our* Super Account Manager (SAM) software. This picture will help us see where in the system we could make improvements that would meet Jason's criteria for perfect accounting software: security, reliability, and flexibility.

Like any visual thinking challenge, we start by *looking,* so here we've compiled a list of all main SAM components. Although the list is categorized, it's impossible to see the relationships between the components.

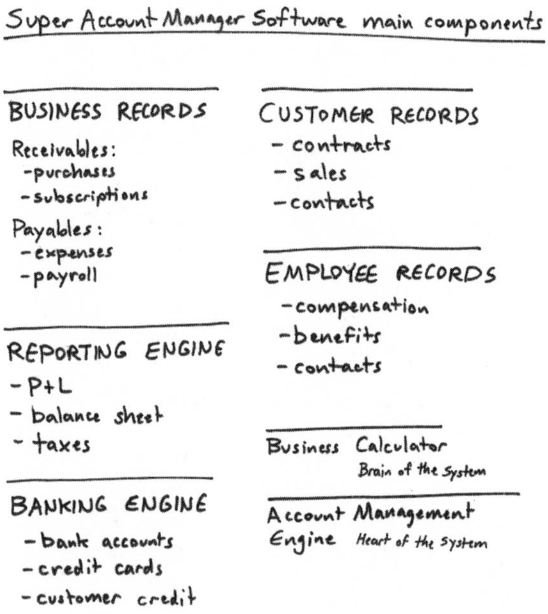

<u>Super Account Manager Software main components</u>

BUSINESS RECORDS

Receivables:
- purchases
- subscriptions

Payables:
- expenses
- payroll

REPORTING ENGINE
- P+L
- balance sheet
- taxes

BANKING ENGINE
- bank accounts
- credit cards
- customer credit

CUSTOMER RECORDS
- contracts
- sales
- contacts

EMPLOYEE RECORDS
- compensation
- benefits
- contacts

Business Calculator
Brain of the System

Account Management
Engine   Heart of the System

Components of our software: a complete list, but impossible to see relationships.

We know that the best way to start a map is to draw in the most prominent feature. In this case, the last item on the list, Account Management Engine, says "the heart of the system," which sounds promising. So if it really is the heart, draw it in the center.

Start with the heart.

The heart of any system connects to all the main components, so let's draw the category titles around it. There seems to be something parallel about employee records (Employees) and customer records (Customers), so draw those at the same level; the same holds true for reporting engine ("Reporter") and banking engine ("Banker").

Concept model of Super Account Manager Software

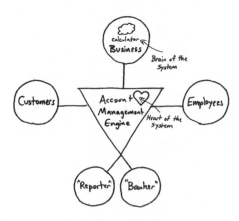

Then we add in the main categories arrayed around the heart.

OK, there's one way of looking at the basic components of our software—and it looks a lot like that conceptual Venn diagram, only there are more parts and they don't overlap as much. Now that we've got the main categories, we can add subcomponents arrayed off those. And as we do, connections between components, which were invisible in the original list, begin to appear.

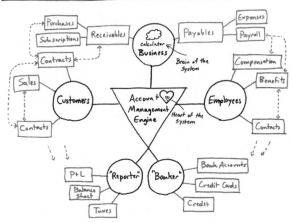

Adding the the subcomponents gives us a complete schematic diagram of our software. We even see connections emerging that were invisible in the original list.

Now that we've got a way to really look at our software package, let's map in areas that we'd need to improve to meet increasing customer demands. To improve security, we'd need to enhance protection around those areas where the most information enters and leaves the system: the "Banker" components that link to separate systems and the banks, and the "Reporter" components that present information to password-protected Web sites.

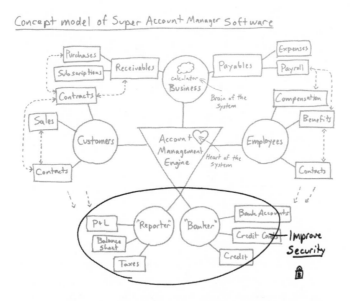

In order to meet executives' demands for more security, we'd need to modify the "Banker" and "Reporter" sections of our application.

Similarly, we can now clearly indicate those components we'd need to modify in order to improve reliability, namely the Business Calculator and the Account Management Engine.

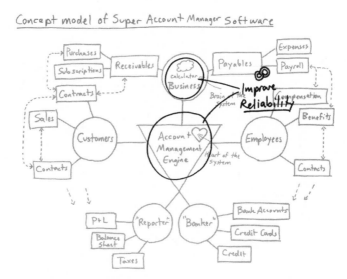

To meet the accountants' demands for improved reliability, we need to modify the Business Calculator ("the brain of the system") and the Account Management Engine ("the heart of the system").

Most important, from Jason's perspective anyway, we can now also use this map of our system to determine where we'd need to make improvements to flexibility. As we can see, there are a lot of areas where the various components interact, and it's in those connections that we can make the biggest changes.

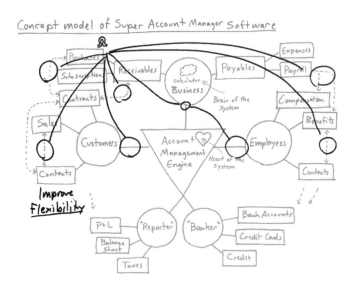

Where Jason would like to see us make improvements: Any way we can simplify and standardize the connections between system components will help flexibility.

There we have it: If we want to make changes to our software, we'll want to start with those areas. These maps show us not only where we should focus improvements on our software, they also show how complex the integration of our system is. In order to make so many changes, we're going to have to undertake a major project—something taking months to complete. In the next chapter on timelines, we'll look at how long such a project would take and *when* we'd need to complete each step.

CHAPTER 12

WHEN CAN WE FIX THINGS?

PICTURES THAT SOLVE A *WHEN* PROBLEM

Framework 4: *To show a* **when problem, use a timeline.**

One Step at a Time

We can now see where changes to our software might make the software more appealing to our biggest buyers. Assuming that we can convince our own management that making those changes is the right way to increase sales (a huge assumption, but one we'll be dealing with when we get to the *why* framework), the next question is how long it is going to take. Will it take a couple weeks, a few months, or a year or more to make these upgrades? Clearly, we're now facing a *when* problem, which the codex tells us to address with a timeline.

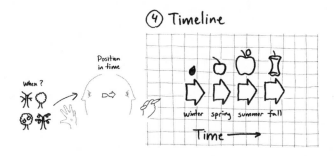

④ Timeline

Position in time

When ?

winter spring summer fall

Time ⟶

Framework type	What it shows	Coordinate system	Objects' relationship	Starting point	Example
4. Timeline	When	now time future	Objects' positions in time	Beginning OR End	Release process

After we saw *where*—and as some time passed—we saw objects change in any of the three previous ways: in quality, in amount, or in position. In order to show those changes to somebody else, we use a timeline to represent the various states of our object at various times, or the relationship of those objects over time.

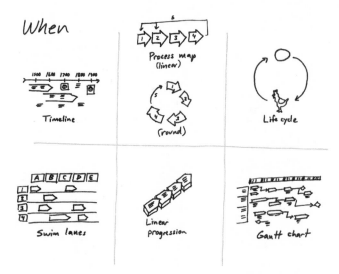

Life cycles, process maps, Gantt charts, progressions, swim lanes: Timelines can take many forms, but they all show the same thing— *when* one activity takes place in time in relation to another.

Timelines: General Rules of Thumb

1. Time is a one-way street. Although discussions about the fourth dimension and the fundamental nature of time can be fascinating, they're irrelevant to the types of problems typically faced in business. For our purposes, we're going to think of time as a straight line that always leads from yesterday to tomorrow, and always tracks from left to right. Although the former rule may not be true for time travelers and the latter is nothing more than a cultural bias, both are useful as standards that we can all recognize and agree on.

2. Repeating timelines create life cycles. Chickens and eggs, up-and-down marketing cycles, days into months into years—timelines frequently repeat over and over again. When they do, we call them life cycles and represent them either as an endless circle or as a returning "back to the beginning" arrow placed at the end of the line. For our purposes, it doesn't matter if the timeline repeats or not, we create it in the same way.

If we can't identify the starting point, we pick a major milestone anywhere along the length of the cycle and begin there.

3. **Round versus linear.** Both a clock and a ruler are made up of a single line, the first one just happens to curve back on itself. While circular timelines are in many ways a more accurate representation of a repeating life cycle, it is almost invariably better to go with a straight line. It's not only easier to draw (especially when the steps are accompanied by detailed text), it's cognitively easier to read, and easier to remember. Circular timelines and calendars (like those of the ancient Aztecs and modern astrologers) are wonderful if your fundamental point is to emphasize the repetitive nature of a particular cycle, but even then it is advisable to create a straight-line version so that you can add details.

To make a SAX Inc. project timeline, we need to start with a coordinate system. And since a timeline shows the relationship of things over time, that's easy. We start at the present and show the passage of time as we move to the right. Since we at SAX have been developing software for a long time now and know exactly how to get started, let's start this timeline at the beginning: discovery.

At SAX Inc. we begin every project by determining what the general problem is that we need to address. We call this the "discovery" phase, and we're already a long way down that path: finding a way to make our accounting software more appealing to Jason.

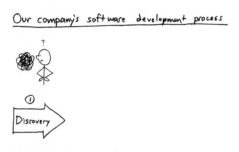

We begin every software development project with "discovery," when we nail down what the problem is that we're trying to solve.

Once we've got a good handle on the problem, we start coming up with possible solutions. We call this "conceptual design," and this is when we nail down the specifics of what we're going to build.

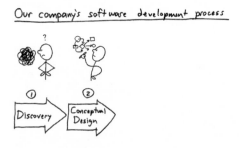

In "conceptual design" we figure out our solution and nail down what it's going to look like.

With the solution designed, we've got to build it. That's where "development" comes in: writing the code, both for all the individual software subcomponents and for the entire application.

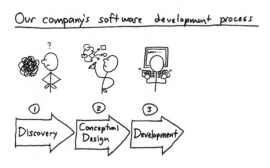

"Development" is when we write the code and create the application.

Once everything is written, it has to be tested . . . and tested, and tested again. That's why the next phase is nothing but testing: bug testing, first-round testing, testing with a small group of customers, and finally user-acceptance testing with a larger group.

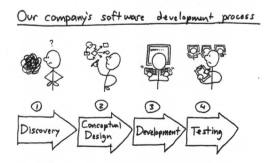

The fourth phase is when we test and test and test again to make sure our application does what it's supposed to do.

With testing complete and all the bugs worked out, we're ready to start selling. We call this final phase "deployment," because this is when we package up our software and get it into the hands of our customers for their use. It's also when we hand over the application to our user support organization so that we can go back and start working on the next version.

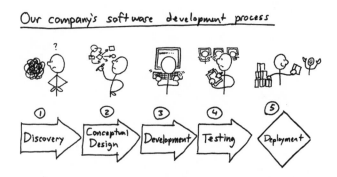

"Deployment" means we start selling the software to customers and turn everything over to the user support group. Our development process is complete.

That's it: our software development timeline. That was a *simple, qualitative, execution-oriented, individual, as-is* view—just the thing that the SQVID tells us to create if our audience is new to the software industry and interested in seeing the big steps. It's a useful starting point, but here we need to get a lot more detailed if we're really going to implement the timeline. So let's take that simple overview as a starting point but redraw it, this time with a focus on the *complex* and *quantitative*. Here we go with the same timeline, but with a different intent in mind.

The first thing that was missing in the previous timeline was that it didn't accurately reflect time. It showed the steps over time, but didn't represent how long any of the five phases actually took. So the first thing we have to do is lengthen the phase arrows to show relative duration—something we know from having completed this same process many times before.

SAX Inc. software release project plan

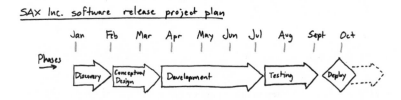

The five phases take differing amounts of time to complete, with development more than double the length of any other.

Past experience gives us a good estimate of how many weeks and months each phase realistically takes to complete, so now we can map in a calendar.

SAX Inc. software release project plan

Adding in a calendar makes the timeline more accurate.

There will be a lot of people working on this project, so let's create a list of project teams and run them down the side, where we'll be able to plot in their individual activities for each phase.

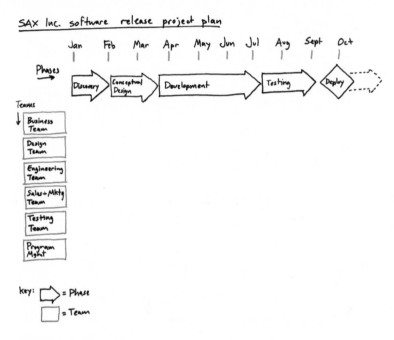

We add in the project teams down the side so we'll be able to plot in their individual activities during each phase.

We've now got two coordinates set up, just as we did on the charts and maps before, but this time we've also got two different *kinds* of information represented on the same playing field: *who* (our teams) and *when* (our timeline). With those two coordinates in, we can start plotting in the *whats,* starting with the critical milestones that mark the close of one phase and the beginning of another.

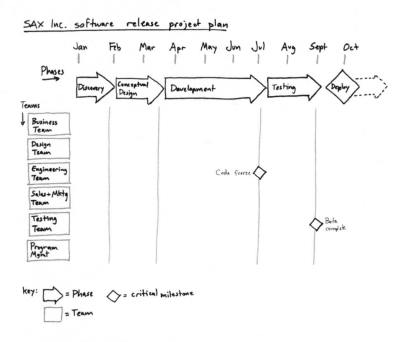

By plotting in critical milestones, we show the triggers that indicate the close of one phase and the beginning of another.

How do we know when we've actually hit one of these milestones? Milestones aren't physical things, they're just predefined moments in time. The way we know we've succeeded in meeting them is by measuring what we've actually gotten done—in the case of a project, those physical things are the "deliverables." For example, once the business team has completed its "business rationale" document, the design team its "user need study," and the sales and marketing team its "market study," we can say that the problem-defined milestone has been reached, and we can begin conceptual design.

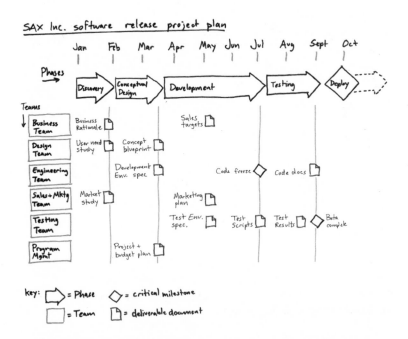

Plotting in the individual team deliverables indicates what physically needs to be completed in order to meet a milestone, to say that one phase is finished and the next really ready to start.

Valuable as they are in content, deliverables are simply the end results of all the heavy lifting that went into them. While seeing when the deliverables are due is critical to planning, we also need to see what is required to create them. That's where work streams come in: They are the task lists of things to do that each team follows in order to know what to do to get their deliverables done. Mapping in the work streams completes this more detailed timeline so that we can now see how long this project is going to take.

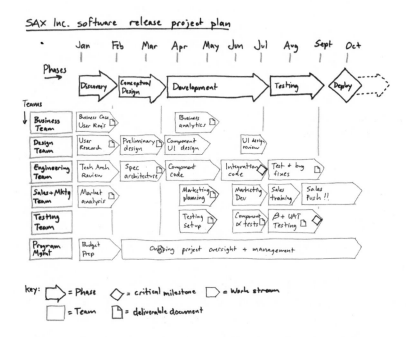

By drawing in each team's work stream, we finally see everything that needs to take place to complete our project, and how long it's going to take: 9 months.

Nine months from the green light to rolling software out the door to customers: We now see how big a commitment of time it is to complete an upgrade to our application. At the million dollars a month it costs to cover salaries and expenses for all team members, that brings us to $9 million. That's a big "ask" at a company our size, so before we go to our own execs, let's see how $9 million compares with the cost of previous development cycles.

To see this, we're going to call upon our first hybrid framework, the time series chart. This is something we haven't seen yet but that will nevertheless be familiar—it's simply a combination of a *how much* chart overlaid on a *when* timeline, two frameworks that we already know well. As the name describes, a time series chart plots the quantity of something changing over time. This framework merges the coordinate systems of its two underlying frameworks in order to show the rise and fall of prices, rates, numbers, temperatures—anything that can be measured at one time and then at another.

Time series

how much + when = amount / time

A time series chart is a superimposition of a timeline axis onto a typical *how much* chart: It shows the variations in quantity of something over time.

Creating a time series chart lets us see how the cost of completing a full software-development cycle now compares with what it has cost in the past. If we're going to be asking for $9 million, we'd better know up front if that's more or less than before. If less, it should be relatively easy to get; if more, we'll have to make an extra-solid case for the project.

Just as in any other timeline, the horizontal coordinate shows time, and as in any other chart, the vertical coordinate shows amount. With those coordinates in place, we can start plotting in development costs from previous years, data we can collect from previous project management files. SAX Inc. opened its doors with its first version of Super Account Manager back in 1996, so let's start there. In that first year, it cost less than $500,000 to create SAM version 1, with a team of ten people working nights and weekends for nearly a year. The cost of the second version, launched two years later, quadrupled to $2 million. The simple reason: The team had grown to forty people, and more people cost more money. By 2000, it cost nearly $6 million to release SAM 3, the version that made SAX Inc. an industry leader.

Then came the bust. In late 2001, the entire market came down, and SAX Inc. had to lay off staff just to stay afloat. We managed to keep releasing upgraded versions of SAM, but development costs went down because teams got smaller and the company became less ambitious with each release.

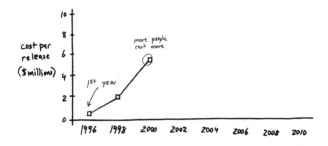

This time series compares development costs to release cycles every two years. At the beginning of SAX Inc. in 1996, it cost $500,000 to create the original application. Two years later it cost four times that, and two years after that it had risen again—to $6 million.

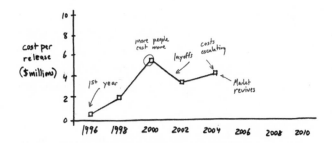

Boom: With the collapse of the market, development costs dropped due to layoffs, then started to rise again as the market recovered in 2004.

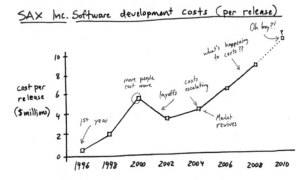

Since 2004, development costs have risen consistently with every release. So if we go ahead with a $9 million version now, we'll be right on track.

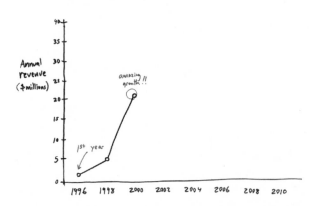

Let's build the same time series but show company revenue rather than project costs, obligating us to slide the vertical scale up to $40 million.

Since then, development costs have increased for every release. SAM 6, which came out in 2006, came in at over $6 million, topping the previous maximum set back in 2000. Given the trends since 2002, it appears that a $9 million cost is right in line with where we'd expect costs to be.

But that doesn't tell the entire story. Much as we'd love to go to our execs and ask for $9 million, showing them this time series chart to justify the cost, we know they're going to ask us to show them something we ourselves haven't uncovered yet: How do these costs track with the overall revenue of the company?

To figure that, we're going to create another time series chart using exactly the same horizontal timeline, only this time the vertical axis will reflect total company revenue, which means we're going to have to slide that scale from $10 million at the top (the highest ever spent on a release) to $40 million, the highest revenue. Once again, we start plotting in numbers in 1996, when total company revenue was about $1 million, through the next four years, when revenues skyrocketed up to $21 million.

Again we see the bubble burst in 2001: Over the next two years revenue drops by more than half, and even after the market recovers we're still sliding down.

In 2004 revenues bounce back with a vengeance, jumping up to $30 million in two years. Then ... well, then we just sit there: flat sales, flat revenue. Which brings us back to the problem that got us started way back with the *who/what* framework.

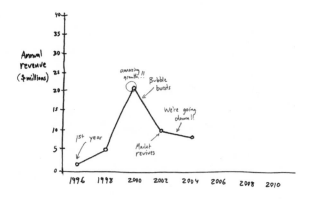

In 2001 revenue heads south and keeps going, even after the market starts coming back.

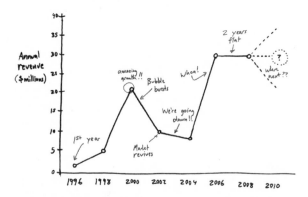

There was massive revenue growth in 2004–2006, and then it all stopped.

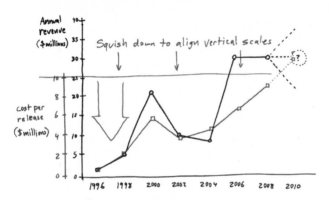

SAX Inc. total annual revenue

Annual revenue ($millions)

Squish down to align vertical scales

Cost per release ($millions)

1996 1998 2000 2002 2004 2006 2008 2010

After we lay the first chart onto the second, we have to squish it down to make the vertical numbers align.

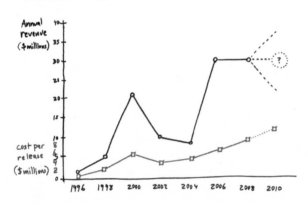

SAX Inc. total annual revenue

Annual revenue ($millions)

Cost per release ($millions)

1996 1998 2000 2002 2004 2006 2008 2010

One chart lays out development costs and revenues side by side, where we can easily compare one with the other.

Viewed individually, these two charts tell us two things: The first showed that development costs are going up at what appears to be a consistent rate; the second shows that revenues (although still high) have flattened. But it's when we put the two together that the real insights—and questions—emerge. To put the two together, we have to do a little fancy footwork. Since the vertical scales were different, we're going to have to squish the costs chart down across the board to align the numbers.

With the scales aligned, we can compare apples to apples and see how development costs have varied compared to revenues.

And we can already hear the execs' response to our $9 million request: *If four years ago a 30 percent increase in costs brought about a 300 percent increase in revenues, but another 30 percent increase two years ago coincided with flat revenues, who's to say another 30 percent increase in costs is going to help at all?*

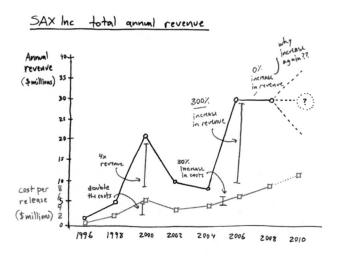

Good question: Revenues aren't going up, so why should costs?

We see the question we're going to have to answer, now we've got to figure out how to answer it.

CHAPTER 13

HOW CAN WE IMPROVE OUR BUSINESS?

PICTURES THAT SOLVE A *HOW* PROBLEM

*Framework 5: To show a **how** problem, use a **flowchart**.*

How Can We Fix This?

We're facing yet another new problem: How are we going to convince the executives (*how are we going to convince ourselves*) that spending $9 million to improve our software is the right way to get sales moving again? Let's face it: Jumping from the desires of the last guy on the org chart to a $9 million spend is a pretty big leap, isn't it?

Stated that way, it is. But maybe that's not the right way to state it. In fact, let's not state it at all: Let's *show* how we came to that conclusion.

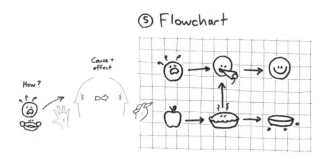

Framework type	What it shows	Coordinate system	Objects' relationship	Starting point	Example
5. Flowchart	*How*	◇——▷□ Action Response	Objects' influences upon each other	◇- - -▷□ Beginning Action Response	Business Work flow

As we saw the ways in which objects interacted over time—changing in quality, number, or position, but now with visible influences upon each other—we saw cause and effect come into play: we saw how things work. The codex tells us that when we need to show such cause and effect, we create a flowchart.

But let's not start with a flowchart as elaborate as the one we'll need to visually link Jason's software desires to a complete rewrite of our platform. Let's practice with a simpler (but equally useful) one. Let's look at how executives in our company go about making such a big financial decision.

The table of frameworks tells us that the coordinate system of a flowchart runs from *action* to *response,* and that the starting point should always be the beginning action. So we'll start with the first thing an exec will say when we show up with our spreadsheets: "Is your problem defined?" followed by, "Have you thought of any potential solutions?"

Knowing that if our answer to either of those queries is no, we'll be shown the door, we'll then pull out our problem definition and proposed sample solutions.

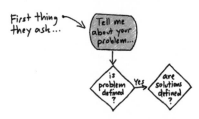

How company decisions are made, part 1: First, the exec will ask us to tell him or her about our problem.

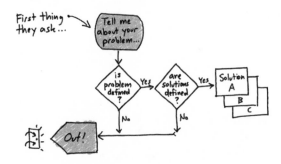

Part 2: If neither the problem nor any potential solution is defined, the conversation is over. On the other hand, if we have some possible solutions, the exec will be all ears.

Then comes discussion of the solutions: Are they technically possible? If no, forget it. If yes, are they then financially reasonable? Again, if not, it's back to the drawing board. But if yes, then comes the acid test: the "gut check." Our execs have been in the software business for a long time and have a good sense of what can really work and what probably won't. So they then ask themselves, "Will what I'm seeing here really fix the problem?" Then they start really thinking.

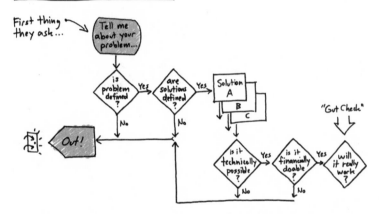

If our proposed solutions are neither technically nor financially feasible, they're rejected. But if they pass on those fronts, they face the biggest test of all: the "gut check."

If the exec's gut tells him or her there is at least a three-quarters' chance of success, he or she gives the green light, and then we're off and running.

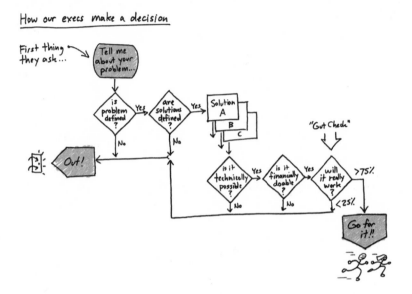

If it feels as if our solution has a 75 percent chance of working, we're off and running. If not, we'd better come up with something else.

Now we know what we're going to face when we go into the big conference room to make our pitch. First thing we'll need is a well-defined problem and an accompanying potential solution. So let's again illustrate our understanding of the original problem using the same flowchart process, but this time things will be a lot more complex—and even our starting point is bad news: flat sales.

We can come up with at least three potential reasons for flat sales: First, our clients aren't themselves growing (which isn't true; they're all growing at least 20 percent per year for the past two years), or they don't need our software anymore (also not true; ours is the most comprehensive product in a growing industry and it will be at least a year before any competitors offer a similar full range of services). No, the only other likely reason is that customers are simply uninspired by our product.

How-to PART I: How do we look at the problem?

start here

Sales are → flat

□ rising
✗ flat
□ falling

We've got to define our problem. In this case, it's big and obvious: Sales aren't rising, but they aren't falling either—no, they're just plain flat.

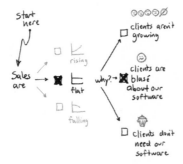

How-to PART I: How do we look at the problem?

start here

Sales are → flat

□ rising
✗ flat
□ falling

why? → ✗ clients are blasé about our software

□ clients aren't growing

□ clients don't need our software

The most reasonable explanation for flat sales is that customers just aren't inspired by our product anymore.

We can think of two possible reasons for our clients to feel blasé about us: Either our software isn't making them happy or we're not targeting the right clients. Both could well be true. Interestingly, addressing both requires the same thing—a better understanding of who our customers are and a better understanding of what they want.

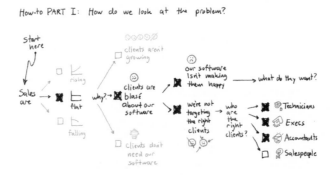

We suspect that our clients aren't happy with our product *and* that we're not targeting the right clients. The good news is that getting a better understanding of who they are should tell us more about what they're looking for.

It's at this point that we created that customer portrait so many pictures back, so now we do know who our influential customers really are (technicians, especially Jason, and execs, and, to a lesser degree, the accountants themselves) and we've identified what they want from accounting software: flexibility, security, and reliability. This brings us to a possible solution: If we improve any one of those three features of our software— especially flexibility, since that's what Jason is really interested in—we should be able to increase sales again.

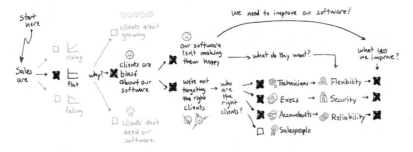

We've got a potential solution: If we improve our software's flexibility, we should be able to inspire Jason to buy more software.

Step one of our executive pitch is ready: We've got the problem clearly defined and we have a potential solution ready. The only trouble is that our solution will cost $9 million. Now we've just got to convince the execs that it's worth it.

CHAPTER 14

WHY SHOULD WE EVEN BOTHER?

PICTURES THAT SOLVE A WHY PROBLEM

Framework 6: To show a **why** *problem, use a* **multiple-variable plot.**

Why Spend the Money?

We're confident that the best way to get sales growing again is to spend the $9 million to rebuild our software platform. Only that ground-up approach will enable us to make the software improvements demanded by our most influential customers. But the fact remains that we could spend a lot less money by making smaller improvements to our existing platform. And with our executives focused intently on the bottom line these days, that's very likely the decision they'll make.

To see why we should make the spending decision one way or the other, we're going to have to look at our entire industry: who our competitors are and their growth projections, how customers and sales trends are changing, and how changes in platform technology will impact revenues. It's only through seeing all that information tied together that the picture we need will emerge. But how can we see all that? Is it even possible to plot together that much information in a meaningful way?

The codex tells us that the coordinate system of a multiple-variable plot is, by definition, composed of three or more variables. Here we have five or six potentially meaningful variables, so let's go ahead and see what happens when we superimpose them onto a single picture. We'll be drawing an *elaborate, quantitative, visionary, comparative, as-is,* and *could-be* plot, a window into the closed box that is our industry. If we can open that window, it should give us a persuasive visual argument for *why* we need to spend the money now.

REVIEW: A MULTIPLE-VARIABLE PLOT SHOWS *WHY*

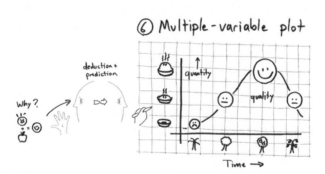

Framework type	What it shows	Coordinate system	Objects' relationship	Starting point	Example
6. Multiple-variable plot	*Why*		Objects' interactions involving any two or more of the above		

After we'd seen *who, what, how much, where, when,* and *how,* we saw reason (or reasons) emerge. The longer we watched everything interact and focused our attention upon cause and effect, the more we began to understand *why* things worked the way they did. In order to show others the reasons and to begin to make predictions about how things will work again, we create multiple-variable plots.

Chapter 5 told us that we see *why* when our mind's eye combines the other ways of seeing. To create a multiple-variable plot we do exactly the same thing, only this time combining them all on a sheet of paper. We start with *who/what,* work through *how much,* shift to *where,* and then add in *when.* Because we've already sketched similar drawings in the previous sections, creating this plot will largely be a review, but with two big differences: First, we'll be layering everything into a single picture rather than separate pictures, and second, we won't start the *who/what* with a portrait of our customers, we'll begin instead with a portrait of our competitors.

Multiple-Variable Plots: General Rules of Thumb

1. **Multiple-variable plots aren't hard to make, but they do require patience, practice, and, above all, a point.** Of the six frameworks and hundreds of picture types out there, a well-thought-through and clearly drawn multiple-variable plot is the most powerful and insightful we can create. (We'll talk about why that's true below.) That said, I can't recall ever seeing a simple explanation in a *business* book of how to draw one. My advice is this: Begin with a simple *x-y* plot, using *any* two qualitative variables for which you have data as the two coordinates (remember, if they turn out to be useless, you can always change them later). Plot in *any* quantitative variable for which you have data using appropriately sized bubbles in the middle, starting with just one point in time. Then add another set of bubbles showing the same quantitative variable at another time. That's it—all you need to complete a multiple-variable plot either as a final picture or as a launching pad for adding more and more variables.

2. **Medium-thick soup is best.** What a multiple-variable plot really does is to create a scale model of an entire business universe or business problem. When we create one, what we're hoping to do is identify a limited number of aspects of our industry (or

problem) that *may* have great influence on one another, so that we can pull out just those and look at them side by side without the distraction of all the other variables out there. Too few variables and we end up with a simple bar chart—useful on its own for many things, but not for developing real insight. Too many variables and we're back to the original problem of too much to look at and we haven't accomplished a thing. Again, the only way to know the "right" number is to start plotting and see when useful ideas emerge.

3. **Anything can be mapped to anything else, but . . .** The biggest danger of multiple-variable plots is that because they invite the layering of many data types, they can make it too easy to "discover" connections between variables that actually have nothing to do with one another. This is the great challenge of statistics and even basic science: keeping "correlation" (the appearance of similar trends between different variables) distinct from "causation" (the direct impact of one variable upon the other). While it may be tempting to map global temperature fluctuations to the frequency of *Bay Watch* reruns—with very possibly a high correlation factor—it does not mean that one necessarily causes the other.

Back to SAX Inc. In our industry, we face two categories of competitors: the old guard (that's us—SAX Inc., along with SMSoft and Peridocs, companies that we've competed with for the past decade) and the new arrivals (Univerce and MoneyFree, which just appeared on the scene a couple years ago). The two groups are further differentiated according to other specific criteria: We big three have all been in business for at least ten years, have all built our software on proprietary code and platforms, all offer software with lots of features, and all make our money through the sales of our software products, throwing in the upgrades and service for free. The smaller two companies built their software using open-source code, have few features, and make their money from support contracts only: They give away their software for free, then charge their clients for upgrades and service.

"Old Guard"   **"New arrivals"**

Now we get to be the big guys!

SAX Inc.   SMSoft   Univerce   MoneyFree

Peridocs   vs.

✓ 10+ years old

✓ proprietary platforms

✓ feature-rich software

✓ premium sales price

✓ free upgrades + service

✓ max 3 years old

✓ open-source platforms

✓ few features

✓ free sales price

✓ paid upgrades + service

Portrait of our competitive set, representing two main groups and differentiated by age and differing approaches to the market.

That's it: five companies, two different platforms, two different ways of doing business. Now let's look at a simple numeric comparison to see *how much* revenue each of these companies earned last year. As we map out the companies by size (using proportionately sized bubbles to represent revenue), another trait emerges: The old guard made all the money last year, while the new arrivals barely made a dent. SAX Inc. lead the pack with revenues of $25 million, followed by SMSoft at $20 million and Peridocs at $18 million. Univerce came in at $3 million and MoneyFree made a small blip at $250,000.

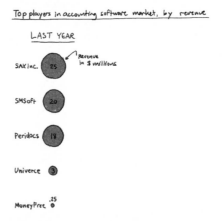

Top players in accounting software market, by revenue

LAST YEAR

SAX Inc.   25   *Revenue in $ millions*

SMSoft   20

Peridocs   18

Univerce   3

MoneyFree   .25

Now let's look forward. Using analysts reports, Wall Street projections, and the industry rumor mill, we can project what revenues are expected to look like among these same companies at the end of next year. We already know that our sales are flat, but here is some new information: SMSoft is in negotiations to buy Peridocs, which will create a combined company with projected revenues of $40 million. On top of that, analysts predict that Univerce, a company that didn't even exist three years ago, will surpass our projected $30 million by more than $1 million, knocking us from first place into third. Even puny MoneyFree will likely bring in $18 million. What?!

That's a lot of industry change in a short period. Aside from the big merger, what else could be happening? Obviously, there's more going on than this simple *how much* chart can show. We need to not only see how big these companies are, we need to see *where* they sit in relation to one another according to customers, platforms, technologies—all those unique variables we identified in our portrait. What we really need is an industry map.

Let's try it. Let's plot together what were otherwise separate pieces of information and see if connections do emerge. The specific pieces that we want to see together are things that we already know: competitor name, type of platform, range of software features, revenue, and time. Remember that a multiple-variable plot overlays three or more different criteria, and to get started we just have to draw in one or two initial axes and give them names. For example, proprietary standards versus open standards plotted against full features versus few features.

Now that we've got an initial coordinate system laid down, this picture becomes like

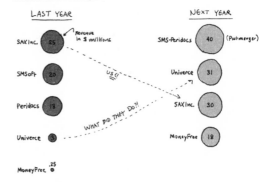

Our competitors' revenues as projected at the end of next year.

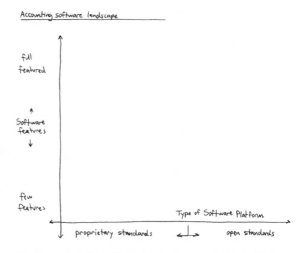

We begin our plot with the horizontal coordinate, in this case type of software platform, then add the vertical software features axis.

any other landscape map, and all we have to do is draw in the features. Since we've already got the bubbles representing last year's revenues ready (our third variable), we can place them in the areas of the plot indicated by the coordinates. For example, SAX, SMSoft, and Peridocs all slide to the proprietary side while the others slide to the open side, and vertically all are arranged according to number of features (SAX has the most, followed by SMSoft, etc.).

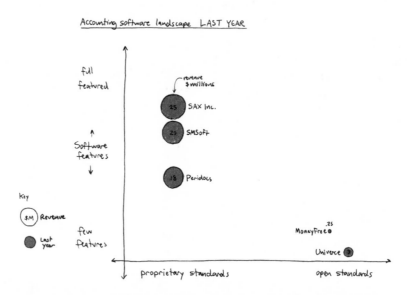

With our coordinates mapped in, we then draw in the features: in this case, the spatial locations of ourselves and our competitors.

So far we're not seeing anything that wasn't already captured by our mind's eye: The big bubbles (more revenue) have more features and are based on proprietary platforms, last year, anyway. We didn't need the picture to tell us that. But when we map in next year's projected data, things jump around—*a lot.*

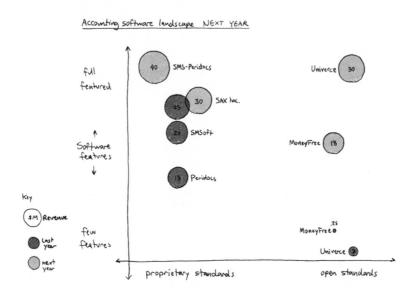

Then we lay in next year's projected revenue, and all the bubbles jump.

Now we've got five variables in play: *name of company, platform, features, revenue last year,* and *revenue next year.* Before we add in more (and we're going to), let's see what we can see. First, the merged SMS-Peridocs surpasses us in revenue (bigger bubble), and their combined software surpasses us in features (their bubble moves up). At the same time, their merger will force them to combine two proprietary platforms, making their platform even less open than before (their bubble moves left). Meanwhile, our revenues have grown slightly (slightly bigger bubble), our continual software tweaks nudge us up a bit in features (our bubble bumps up), and, assuming we go through with planned platform Band-Aids, we are slightly more open (our bubble nudges right).

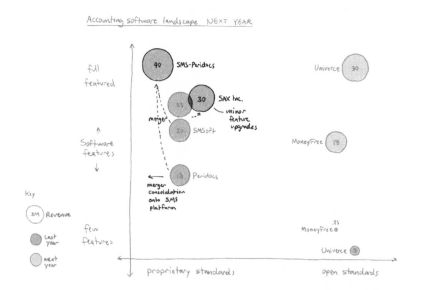

The postmerger SMS-Peridocs surpasses us in revenue and features but becomes an even more proprietary (closed) system, while we marginally increase features and slightly open up our platform.

Meanwhile, let's look at what has happened on the open standards side of the plot. All the sudden revenue increases and feature upgrades of the old guard don't look so impressive. By the end of next year, it's projected that Univerce will not only exceed our revenues, they'll also beat us in number of features. How is that possible?

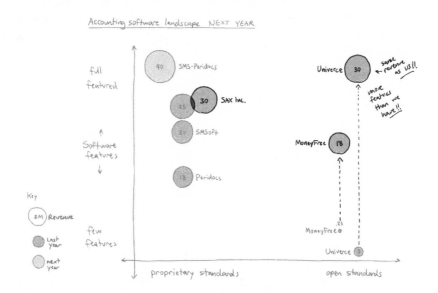

Next year the growth of the old guard pales by comparison to Univerce and MoneyFree, the new arrivals. Suddenly they've got more features and revenue growth than we've ever experienced.

In order to see what's going on, we need to plot in yet another layer of data. But before we do, we're going to need to make some room. Let's erase some of the details we've accumulated so far and pick things up by recalling the software improvements that Jason was demanding from us: flexibility, security, and reliability. In the past, proprietary platforms like ours were more secure and reliable than open platforms, although less flexible. To show that on our plot, we can just divide last year's landscape right down the middle: more secure and reliable on the old guard side (left); more flexible on the new arrivals side (right).

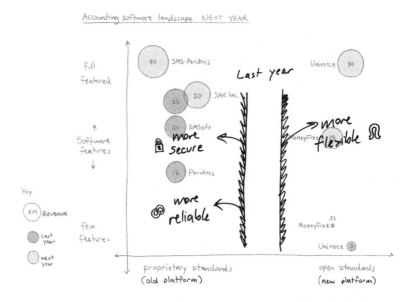

In years past, proprietary platforms were inherently more secure and reliable, while open platforms were generally more flexible.

This is why any Band-Aid increase in flexibility on our platform will decrease security and reliability: We'd be moving our bubble to the right without taking the security/reliability line with us. But over the next couple years, it's expected that open platforms will improve so much that they'll become as secure and reliable as our systems are today—and remain more flexible as well. In other words, the companies with systems built on open platforms are not only going to offer more flexibility, they'll be able to offer as much security and reliablity as those of us with closed systems—if not more so.

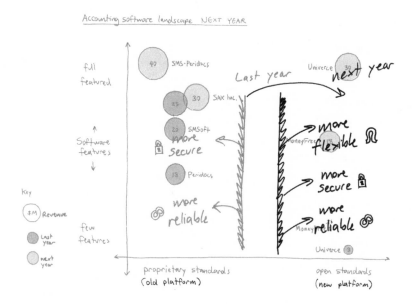

The whole landscape is going to shift next year as open platforms improve. They'll offer security and reliability equal to (if not better than) our closed platform without losing any of their greater flexibility.

We can finally see what's really going on in our industry. As early as next year, the new arrivals—companies that came late and built their systems on open standards—are going to be able to offer services equal to or better than those of us who started early on with our own closed platforms. Which finally brings us back to our original question: Why spend $9 million on building a new open platform when we could spend a lot less on more moderate improvements to the platform we already have?

Believe it or not, we've now collected everything we need to show *why*. We started this chapter with a simple question: *Does knowing anything more about our customers tell us why sales are flat?* Using the six fundamental frameworks of visual thinking, we've not only answered that question (*yes—we're not pleasing Jason*), we've seen exactly how to go about keeping our customers happy (*improve security, reliability, and flexibility*) and stay the leader in our industry (*move to an open platform*). The problem is that it's going to cost $9 million. Which means there remains one more thing to do: Share these pictures with our executives and get them to see the same things we did—to see *why* for themselves.

In the next and final part of this book, we're going to walk through a short executive presentation built around nothing more than the pictures we've just created. In doing so, we'll answer the two remaining "big" questions about visual thinking—those that I am asked every time I talk about solving problems with pictures. First, what's the best way to effectively show a picture? Second, does a good problem-solving picture always have to be self-explanatory?

PART IV
SELLING IDEAS

It's <u>Showtime</u>

CHAPTER 15

EVERYTHING I KNOW ABOUT BUSINESS I LEARNED IN SHOW-AND-TELL

There are two remaining big questions about visual thinking, tough questions I'm asked every time I talk about solving problems with pictures. Both relate to selling ideas with pictures, the time when we need to finally share with somebody else the pictures we've created. The first question has to do with us as presenters: How can we best go about verbally describing a picture? The second has to do with our pictures themselves: Are they "bad" if they require any explanation at all?

Everything I Know about Business I Learned in Show-and-Tell

Walk into a kindergarten class and (with the teacher's permission) ask for a show of hands on how many of the six-year-olds can sing. Every hand will go up in the air. How many can dance? Every hand. How many can draw? Every hand. Now ask how many can read: a couple hands might rise. Then walk into a tenth-grade classroom and ask the sixteen-year-olds the same questions: How many can sing? One or two hands. How many can dance? A few. How many can draw? A couple. Now ask how many can read. Every hand will go up.

Don't get me wrong: There's certainly nothing wrong with learning to read. But what happened to singing, dancing, and drawing? Once we believed that we knew how to do those things—in fact, at kindergarten age most of us practiced them happily every day—so why, ten years later, do so many of us forget what we once knew? And by forgetting (or even just thinking we've forgotten), are we missing something fundamental in our innate problem-solving abilities that could be useful to us in the black-and-white, right-and-wrong, quantitative world of business?

As we reach the end of this book, I have one final story to share, and it's the best example ever of how *not* to present a problem-solving picture. It's a scary story and on the surface may appear to undermine much of what we've talked about here—at least that's what I thought when it took place. Only on reflection did I come to realize that the story, in fact, makes the case for visual thinking stronger, especially since addressing it forced me to go back and look at my approach to visual thinking all over again.

A year ago, I was hired to join a team of business consultants working on a huge technology project sales pitch. Each member of this team was handpicked for his or her proven expertise in a particular field, and each had been all over the world selling and leading successful projects. As I stepped into the conference room to meet them for the first time, I was already impressed. If you planned to spend $100 million on a new enterprise-wide technology system, these were the people you wanted: They just looked *right*.

Although I was brought in to help out just on the charts, I had a wonderful time working with this team, and even succeeded in convincing them to use pictures during key parts of their sales presentation instead of the usual bullet points. Having seen audiences fall asleep after the second page of bullets, the team was all for it, and after nearly three weeks of work we were all amazed by what we'd been able to accomplish. Together we'd managed to boil down a hundred pages of material into just six handouts and a dozen slides, without compromising any of the core materials and without losing the overall storyline of the proposal.

The showpiece of the presentation was a multiple-variable plot similar to the one we just created for SAX Inc. It illustrated the client's industry by mapping together several variables (competitors, market share, industry work flow, sales over time) that were individually familiar to the audience but had never before been seen together in one place. The result was a picture that offered up numerous insights. It showed that the client's business model placed them at several unconnected steps across their industry; it showed that while they led in two of those steps, they lagged in others; it showed that their biggest competitors focused on dominating only single steps, etc. In other words, it was a picture that could launch any of several fascinating conversations, all of which were important to the client's decision-making process and all of which the team was prepared to run with.

As the chart guy, I didn't have a speaking part on pitch day, so I was given the unfamiliar role of sitting in the back of the auditorium where I could judge audience response and take notes for debriefing later. When our team entered the auditorium to deliver the pitch, I was ready to be amazed. I was, but not for the reasons I'd expected.

Lauren, the team leader, opened the pitch brilliantly. She was a great speaker— charming, engaging, *loud*. She led with a funny anecdote that got a chuckle from the room full of client executives, technologists, and finance people. It couldn't have been a better start.

But then she hit the "next slide" button, looked up at the multiple-variable plot with its four layers of seamlessly integrated visual information, precognitive attributes, intuitive coordinate system . . . and froze.

It was like watching a cartoon: Lauren's mouth opened but nothing came out; her eyes darted across the fifteen-foot projection screen but saw nothing. As Lauren stood there, hands locked in midgesture, the room held its breath, waiting for her to explain what they were looking at, what it meant, and why they should care. But no sound was heard. I twisted in my seat, agonizing, barely able to keep from shouting out, *"Lauren! Just say what this chart shows and start pointing!"*

Mercifully, I managed to remain silent, and Lauren—the consummate consulting professional—wasn't going to let a bunch of colored bubbles on a chart knock her off track for long. She took a breath, recovered her composure, and said, "We created this chart to show where you sit in your industry. Next slide please."

We didn't win the project.

In the debrief we all agreed on what had happened: Although Lauren and the team now knew how to create a problem-solving picture, we'd never discussed how to *talk* about one. When she got up on stage in presentation mode, Lauren's mind expected the slides behind her to contain words in lists, something that she'd spoken to hundreds of times. But when she turned around and saw colored balls and bits of text connected by lines and arrows, her mind went blank. Where was she supposed to start? What was she supposed to say? Other than the headline and the labels on the coordinates, there was nothing there to read: no bullet points, no summary, no *words*.

I knew at that moment I'd stumbled upon the greatest challenge to solving problems with pictures: Although we know how to *look*, to *see*, to *imagine*, and to *show*, nobody since kindergarten has told us how to *talk* about what we see. Just like singing, dancing, and drawing, we once knew how to *show* and *tell*, and we did it without bulleted lists. Not anymore.

For a time, I despaired: Was there no future for anything other than simple tables, Venn diagrams, and bar charts as presentation tools? How could that be, after all my research and personal experience in seeing how well pictures worked? Then I remembered the English breakfast and the countless other pictures I'd worked on with teams across dozens of companies in half a dozen countries, the pitches I'd seen won based on nothing more than a single chart that the CEO immediately "got," and the project teams that understood what they were supposed to do only when they'd reviewed that detailed Gantt chart. No, I thought, the problem isn't with the pictures—the problem is in remembering that *show* and *tell* are two different words.

Then it hit me: We already have the answer, and just like the visual thinking process itself, the answer is something we all do all the time without even being aware of it. In fact, the process for talking about a picture *is* the visual thinking process. Let me show you what I mean. Let's go back to SAX Inc. for a moment, and make that final $9 million pitch to the executives.

Look, See, Imagine, Show: The Four Steps of Selling an Idea with a Picture

Quick review: We've created a series of pictures to help us solve the problem of flat sales at our accounting software company, SAX Inc. Those pictures lead us to a possible solution—spend $9 million to completely rebuild our software platform. OK, that's one problem solved, another created. How are we going to convince our executives to spend $9 million on a major project when we have flat sales? To address that, we created another set of pictures. We mapped our executives' decision-making process, exposing cause and effect with a flowchart so we could see what we'd need to show, and then we prepared an *elaborate, quantitative, visionary, comparative, forward-thinking* picture to tell them the whole story.

Imagine that we've scheduled a meeting to present our ideas to the execs. We're in the conference room thirty minutes early, preparing for the execs to arrive. No worries. The way we're going to approach this is exactly the same way we made our pictures: We are going to take the execs with us through the four-step visual thinking process as we *look* at a landscape of information, *see* those things in it that matter most, *imagine* what they mean, and then *show* the result. The only difference is this time the information landscape is a plot we've already created, and we already know exactly what we want to show.

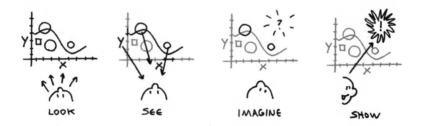

Look, see, imagine, show. We've done it before and now we'll do it again.

As we're waiting for the execs, we're not booting up our computers, looking for wireless connectivity, or trying to hook up the projector that never shows the right resolution, but that doesn't mean we don't have pictures to show. And we're not stacking up color-printed decks in front of each seat, but that doesn't mean we don't have sheets and data to hand out at the appropriate time. No, what we're doing is drawing our picture on the whiteboard, as big as we can. We're sketching in the coordinates and first four variables of our plot *(competitors, platform, features, last year's revenue)*, preparing to convince our execs *why* by engaging them in an interactive (truly back and forth), live (but that doesn't mean unscripted), back-to-basics (but that doesn't mean simplistic) visual thinking session.

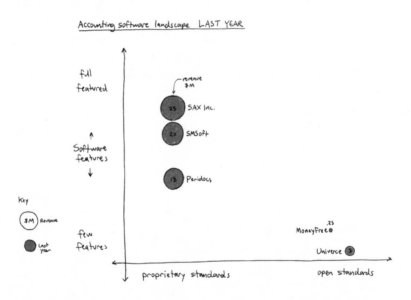

This is what we draw on the whiteboard *before* the execs come into the room—the title, coordinates, key, and first five variables of the plot.

With our drawing done, we sit down and take a breath. Right on time, the execs arrive. Our execs don't like small talk these days, so we stand up and immediately direct their attention to the whiteboard.

"As we all know, we've got a major problem to solve. Sales of SAM have flattened, and if we don't get sales back up in the next year, we stand to lose our top spot in the market. Our group believes that we've identified a solution, and we want to share it with you by taking you through this visual overview of our market."

Brief aside. The fact that we've got an elaborate picture drawn up on the whiteboard is already working in our favor. Since the executives can immediately see that we've got something well thought out in mind, but can't completely understand everything on it, they are anxious to hear what we have to say. They'll likely even give us a moment more than usual to get to the point. This is when we start *looking* aloud.

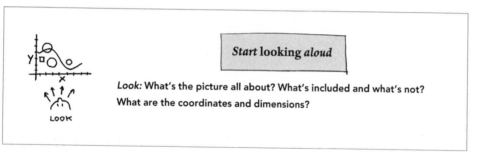

Start looking aloud

Look: What's the picture all about? What's included and what's not? What are the coordinates and dimensions?

Looking aloud means that we aren't going to toss our executives into the middle of the metaphorical bowling alley. We're going to take their hand and walk them there, pointing out the coordinates and dimensions of the place as we go, giving them a moment to figure out where we are and what we're supposed to do now that we're here.

With that approach in mind, we start the tour of our picture. "Our goal in creating this model was to build a baseline of our industry according to several critical factors, ranging from platform to feature set to revenue We believed that by looking at the business in this integrated way we would see our problem in a new light, potentially illuminating new and unexpected approaches to solving it.

"There's a lot included here—and there's going to be a lot more—so let me quickly show you what we have. First, we looked at what types of competitors we face, whether running on proprietary or open systems, which we plotted here along the bottom." *We point out the horizontal axis.*

"Next, we asked what kind of features each company's software offers, whether a full suite or just a few. We plotted that here, going up the side." *We point out the vertical axis.*

"Then we added in last year's revenues using proportionally scaled bubbles plotted onto the appropriate quadrants of the chart. You see us up here in the lead with revenues last year of $25 million and the fullest feature set running on our proprietary platform, while you see MoneyFree way down here, with few features running on an open platform, and next to no revenue." *We point out the bubbles at the extreme ends of the scales.*

We look at the execs and see nods; they're with us so far. Time to let go of their hands and take a step back: We're about to drop a bomb.

Keep seeing *aloud.*

See: **What are the three most important things that stand out? How do they interact? Is there a pattern emerging? Is there anything critical that we don't see?**

Seeing is about pointing out what's most important in the picture—something that we haven't even drawn in. So, as we say, "Here are those same companys' revenues projected for next year," we draw in next year's bubbles starting with our own quadrant, explaining about the SMSoft-Peridocs merger, etc., then draw in MoneyFree, and finally Univerce.

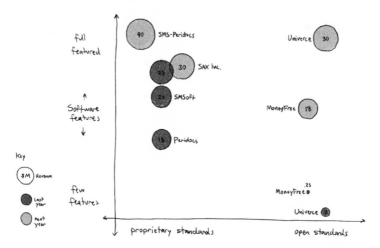

full
featured

SMS-Peridocs 40

Univerce 30

SAX Inc. 30
25

↑
Software
features
↓

SMSoft 20

Peridocs 15

MoneyFree 18

Key

$M Revenue

Last year

next year

few
features

MoneyFree .25

Univerce 3

← proprietary standards   open standards →

↓

One by one we draw in next year's bubbles, starting in our corner and saving Univerce for last.

"Not only is Univerce expected to grow ten times in revenue, it could very likely surpass us in features as well, knocking us into third place in offerings and size." *Boom.*

Our executives see the point now and the questions start to fly. Some are defensive, like, "That can't be right. Where did you get those numbers?" Some are aggresive, like "What in the heck is Univerce up to?" Some are cautiously exploratory, like "Hmm—is there anything we can do?"

The first question we answer precisely because we know exactly where the numbers came from, and that's when we hand out the detailed data spreadsheets we created while researching the picture. The second question we answer by describing next year's anticipated increase in security and reliability on the open platform and the immediate impact that it will have on sales of open software. As for the third question—*"What can we do?"*—we're ready for that one, too. "Thank you for the perfect segue," we respond, "let us take you through two possible options that we've identified."

IMAGINE

Continue by imagining aloud.

Imagine: How can we manipulate or take advantage of emerging patterns? Are there open opportunities? What is not visible here? Where have we seen this before?

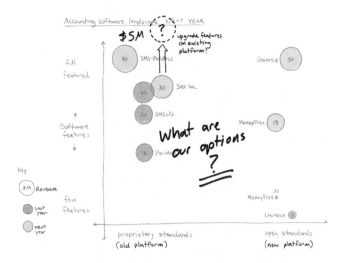

Option one: We explain how spending a little on platform upgrades could likely reestablish our lead in feature offerings, but would have only partial impact on improving overall security, reliability, and flexibility.

Imagining aloud means talking through the options that our picture presents and making the empty spaces come alive. As we introduce option one—the low-cost Band-Aid—we draw in exactly what we're describing, making it obvious that the potential impact of staying on the same platform will be slightly improved services and features—perhaps even enough to keep us ahead of SMS-Peridocs for a time.

Then we draw in option two, describing how a $9 million platform redesign will enable us to make real improvements in all offerings, and position us to stay ahead of the rising open platform crowd—beating them by joining them.

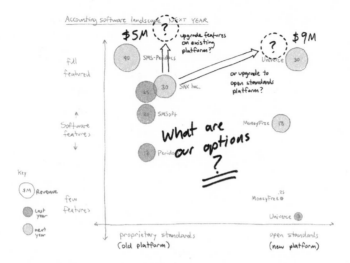

Accounting software landscape NEXT YEAR

$5M · upgrade features on existing platform?

$9M

or upgrade to open standards platform?

full featured

↑
Software features
↓

few features

Universe · 30

SAX Inc.

MoneyFree · 18

SMSoft

SMS-Pentdocs · 40

Peridot

What are our options ?

Key

$M) Revenue

last year

next year

proprietary standards (old platform)

open standards (new platform)

MoneyFree · .25

Universe

Option two: We explain how a $9-million rebuild, using open standards will shift us into leadership on the fastest growing side of the picture.

Now the executives will have one more big question. "OK," they'll say to us, "you've spent a lot of time with this picture, what do you think we should do?"

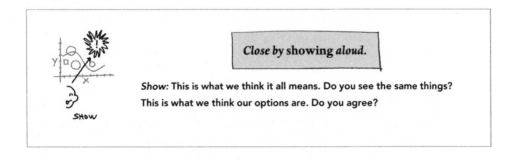

Close by showing aloud.

Show: This is what we think it all means. Do you see the same things? This is what we think our options are. Do you agree?

SHOW

And now we finally come to *why* we need to go with option two and spend the big money: Regardless of our market position today, there is no way we will be able to compete on flexibility, security, and reliability in the coming years on our present platform. Open platforms will simply beat us. We've led this industry for the past decade, and if we intend to keep our lead, there's only one way for us to go: rebuild from the ground up using open standards. As far as we can see, it's not even a question.

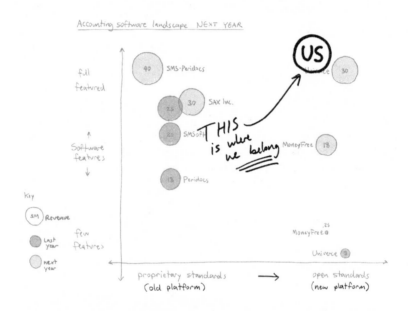

If we want to stay in the lead in the industry we created, we've got no choice but to rebuild on a new open platform.

Our argument is made. The meeting is far from over, but our picture has served its purpose. It introduced more concepts more quickly than we ever could have done with words alone; it made those concepts easy to see, understand, and remember; and it provided a visual framework upon which we and the executives will be drawing more arrows and options for the next hour. Big decisions are about to be made. Let's hope that we've been honest with what we've drawn.

Sometimes a Pizza Is Enough. Sometimes It's Not

The differences in style—and the associated successes—between Lauren's approach to showing her picture during the big pitch and what we just saw in the SAX Inc. conference room are enormous. Still, they all boil down to just one thing: If we're going to use a picture to sell, we have to be prepared to talk about it.

This brings us to the last problem in this book, namely, Is a problem-solving picture "bad" if it requires an explanation? After all, doesn't the old adage "a picture is worth a thousand words" tell us that good pictures always stand on their own?

The answer is no. All good pictures do *not* need to be self-explanatory, but they do need to be *explainable*. It's a rare problem-solving picture of any sort that can carry a clear message, convey powerful meaning, and inspire deep insight without at least a caption. Certainly a basic portrait, bar chart, or simple timeline should be understood immediately, but when we think about the more elaborate and insightful pictures required to show complex interactions of *when, where, how,* and *why,* the point isn't to replace *all* the words; the point is to use a picture to replace those words that are more effectively conveyed, understood, and remembered *visually.*

The best way to think about this is to think about pizza. More to the point, what we really need to think about is when pizza is the ideal food to serve guests versus when a three-course sit-down meal is more appropriate. Here's what I mean. For most business meetings that take place on a day-to-day level, our expectations as participants are usually pretty low. We've met all these people before, heard most of what everybody has to say, and have plenty of other things we could be doing. Those are what I call pizza meetings: They're more like having a bunch of neighbors over to watch a game on TV than having everybody get dressed up to share a gourmet meal. Either way, everybody needs to be fed, but at a pizza meeting the only expectations about the food are that it's filling, tastes pretty good, and doesn't require a lot of cleanup.

Most business pictures are pizza: They need to be simple, easy to digest, and contain few enough ingredients that they don't cause indigestion. These pizza pictures shouldn't need a lot of explanation. They're there to push the meeting forward and get everyone fed on the information as quickly and satisfyingly as possible. More customer data has been collected? Great. Give it to us as a bar chart. A new work stream and deadline have been added to the project? Fine. Where's the one-line timeline? That's it? Great, got it. Thanks. Later.

Then again, a lot of meetings involve a whole different set of expectations. Imagine that we're the new boss and we're meeting the board to relay the impressive results of our first ninety days. Imagine that we've just acquired a new company and we need to convey to senior staff how our business model is going to change; imagine we're meeting a client for the biggest pitch in our company's history. Guests at these meetings expect to be impressed, to learn something they didn't know, to see something they've never seen before . . . and pizza pictures aren't going to cut it.

These meetings are like full-blown sit-down dinners, and the pictures we show need to convey substantial insight, open up interesting conversation, and support important decision making. We're talking here about delivering more than just informational satisfaction. We need to provide the pictorial equivalent of a three-course meal. That's when our elaborate *how* and *why* pictures become the order of the day: They contain a lot, they show a lot, and—as we just saw in the SAX conference room—they require a lot of explanation.

Nothing wrong with that. At our metaphorical sit-down-dinner meeting, our guests not only have more time, they fully expect to be engaged in detailed conversation and are willing to make the commitment of time and energy necessary to ensure they're getting the most from what we've got to show them. *You say we need to think about branching into new international markets? Interesting. What makes you say that? Investing in a new product development now? How could that be? You need nine million dollars? Show me why.*

It's in these instances—when our guests' expectations are high but their willingness to participate is equally high—that we should always pull out the big pictures. The elaborate maps, the comparative timelines, the quantitative value chains, the visionary plots. These pictures serve as launching platforms from which ideas can grow, which is the whole point of problem solving. We don't show an insight-inspiring picture because it saves a thousand words; we show it because it elicits the thousand words that make the greatest difference.

CHAPTER 16

DRAWING CONCLUSIONS

Visual Thinking: The Take-Anywhere Problem-Solving Toolkit

That morning on the train to Sheffield, I not only learned about the power of a napkin, I also learned that what we all really need is a reliable problem-solving toolkit that we can take with us anywhere; something that we can pull out of our pocket at a moment's notice to help us look at problems, see what makes them tick, imagine ways to solve them, and then show our solutions to somebody else. We need a universal visual thinking toolkit—and since we'll be using it at a moment's notice, above all it has to be memorable.

Three-Four-Five-Six: The Visual Thinking Swiss Army Knife

One last visualization exercise. Imagine that you're sitting at the airport café waiting for your flight. You see a couple friends or business colleagues walking past and wave them down. As they join you, they ask what you've been up to lately.

"Solving problems with pictures," you say. "Learning to get better at visual thinking."

"Really?" they say. "What's that all about?"

"Let me show you," you answer as you pick up a napkin and pull a pen from your bag.

As you roughly sketch the outline of a Swiss Army knife, you say, "Picture visual thinking as the Swiss Army knife of problem solving. It has several different blades to help visually solve almost any kind of problem, but they follow a simple pattern so it's easy to remember what they all do."

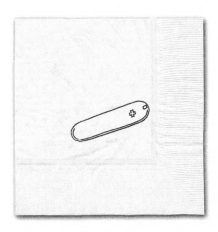

"First are our three basic visual thinking tools: our eyes, our mind's eye, and our hand-eye coordination."

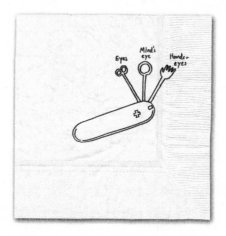

"Next come the four steps of the visual thinking process. Four steps we already know how to do: *look, see, imagine,* and *show.*"

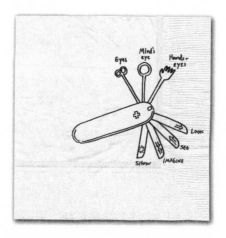

"Then we have the SQVID, the five questions that help us open our mind's eye: simple or elaborate, qualitative or quantitative, vision or execution, individual or comparison, change or status quo?"

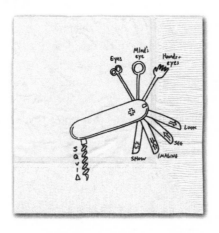

"Last come the six ways we see, and the six corresponding ways we show: *who/what, how much, where, when, how,* and *why.*"

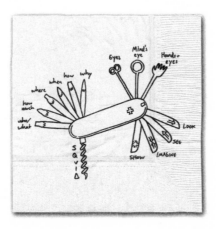

"That's my visual problem-solving toolkit. I don't have to remember any more than that, and I can use it to help with any problem, anytime, anywhere."

"That's pretty interesting," your first colleague says. "I've got a little time . . . can you show me more?"

"Of course" you say, as you reach for another napkin.

"That *is* interesting," says the other colleague. "I want to think about it some more, but I've got to run. Do you mind if I keep the napkin?"

"Not at all," you reply, handing it over with a smile.

In two minutes you've captured your own idea, shown it to others, and passed it along. That's how visual thinking works, and that's how to solve problems and sell ideas with pictures.

ACKNOWLEDGMENTS

STORYTELLERS
People who shared their visual thinking adventures with me.

FRIENDS
People who supported the book from Day One.

APPENDIX A

THE SCIENCE OF VISUAL THINKING

Russian Roulette

This book is what scientists call empirically based. That is to say, I discovered and tested the ideas introduced here during real-world, on-the-job practice and observation, first by trying out visual problem-solving approaches that felt intuitively right, and then by validating that they really did work in solving daily business problems. If I found that a given approach "worked"—by providing either qualitatively better ideas and communications or quantitatively measurable improvements in sales, productivity, or efficiency—I kept evolving it until the tools that appear in this book emerged. If the approaches didn't work, they don't appear here.

For me, there wasn't any alternative to this seat-of-the-pants, learning-by-doing introduction to visual problem solving. In early 1990, I found myself managing a marketing communications company in Russia, a country where I didn't even speak the language. If that sounds like a contradiction in terms (how can someone create communications when they can't speak the language?), it was, but it was also a unique situation that obligated me to start looking for new *nonverbal* ways of approaching business problems.

Those were busy years, and while I eventually learned to speak Russian, I found it more useful to keep using pictures to share ideas even after I'd passed the language barrier. Again, pictures just worked. It never occurred to me to look for any scientific reason why one picture might immediately clarify a complex business issue while another picture would only make the situation worse. I just learned to go by "visual feel." By the time I returned to the United States in the late 1990s, I had seen enough consistently recurring visual themes in the more effective pictures that I learned to quickly create problem-clarifying sketches (like the English breakfast napkin) that other people also found useful—but I never really knew *why* any of those pictures worked.

It was only after I started fine-tuning my approach in order to help colleagues and clients create similar pictures themselves that it dawned on me to look for connections between what I intuitively saw working and what neuroscientists had to say about how human vision works.

Reading about vision in a series of science texts, I started to sense connections emerging, but my own undergraduate degree in biology was by then so dated that those connections remained just out of grasp. Then a client told me about a book called *Phantoms in the Brain: Probing the Mysteries of the Human Mind* by V. S. Ramachandran. I picked up a copy one day and opened it to a chapter on understanding vision. Suddenly I could sense the tumblers whirring in the lock and feel the *click* as a neurological key to visual thinking fell into place.

In his book, Ramachandran (the director of the Center for Brain and Cognition at the University of California, San Diego) presented one fascinating tale after another illuminating the inner workings of the brain. But what caught my eye was a diagram illustrating the *vision pathways*—the neurological routes that visual signals follow as they make their way from our eyes into our visual cortex. When Ramachandran wrote his book in 1998, several recent discoveries had been made delineating these pathways and the roles they appeared to play in breaking down incoming visual signals into the discrete components required for processing throughout the brain. This particular diagram illustrated three of these pathways, and what I saw there was astonishing: Their names matched three of the 6 W's.

I had long ago realized that by visually breaking a problem down into its 6 W's (*who/ what, how much, where, when, how,* and *why*) and then creating a single picture for each, it was possible to visually clarify almost any problem, and yet when faced with the names of these recently discovered visual pathways, I couldn't believe what I saw. The flow of the pathways was itself interesting, but what really took my breath away was their blessedly nonscientific names: the *what* pathway, the *where* pathway, and the *how* pathway. Here were the same "ways of seeing" that I'd always relied upon, but now they weren't abstract ideas to search for in the visual world, they were physical pathways leading directly into specific areas in our brains.

"Wait a minute," I told myself. "It can't be that simple. It can't be that we physically *see* according to the 6 W's—*who, what, when, where, etc.* That would be too easy. Those are just broad journalistic definitions we've made up in order to understand and convey the essence of complex stories, right?"

Wrong. Now intrigued enough to read everything I could find about how vision/sight works, I soon discovered two things: One, there is enough scientific evidence to contemplate the truth of a visual thinking model that says that the 6 W's are the "ideal" way to look at the world because they correspond literally to the ways we see. Two, like anything in science, it's not *completely* true.

How We See, Part I: The Vision Pathways

Way back at the beginning of chapter 4, I described *looking* as the means by which we collect visual information through our eyes. We talked about how light enters our eyes and gets converted into electrical signals that are passed along our optic nerves into various regions of our brains, where those signals somehow get processed into the pictures that we *see* inside our heads. That's an accurate and useful summary to the basics of our visual system, but it barely scratches the surface. Vision is an enigma, a process that becomes ever more remarkable the more neuroscientists learn about it, and yet to this day remains fundamentally a mystery.

What we do know is this: Every second that our eyes are open, millions of visual signals enter as photons of light, are instantly converted into electrical impulses by our retinas, and then get passed along through the million strands of our optic nerves into our brains. After the right-side and left-side eye signals cross over in the optic chiasma, about

10 percent of the signals get shunted along a three-hundred-million-year-old pathway into the superior coliculus located atop the brain stem.

THE OLD PATHWAY

The brain stem is also known as the reptilian brain, so called because it is the ancient core of our brain that we have in common with reptiles; it's the part of our brain responsible for our basic "fight or flight" survival skills. The relatively small number of visual signals captured here in the superior coliculus gets passed on to the pulvinar nucleus for rapid initial processing, and then on to the parietal lobes for final processing. This series of stops is called the old pathway, or the original *where* pathway, because the signals processed here tell us only one thing: *where* stuff is.

Remember when we walked into the bowling alley and our minds instantly "read the room," establishing the coordinates, orientation, and position of we ourselves and the objects around us? That's the job of this old *where* pathway. It doesn't provide any information about *what* we're seeing, or even identify anything by name—all this *where* pathway does is tell us if we're upright or not and whether something is zooming toward us. It doesn't even matter what that something is. If it's approaching, we're going to take action, simple as that.

No wonder reptiles don't seem too smart. The only vision system they have is limited to *where* information; they have no ability to learn to visually recognize and

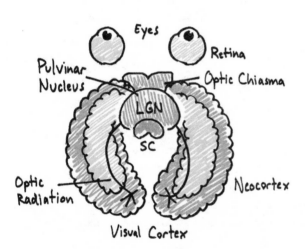

Our *looking* system includes our eyes and many parts of our brain. The older superior coliculus (SC) sits atop the brain stem; the newer lateral geniculate nucleus (LGN) sits astride the neocortex.

"name" the things they see. Try this: Throw a Nerf ball at a (human) friend's head. The first few times he'll duck, but once he realizes it won't hurt him, he'll have no problem standing still as it clobbers him. Now try it with an alligator. Although alligators have been on this planet for three hundred million years longer than people, they'll never figure out that they don't need to dodge Nerf balls. They'll flinch no matter how many times you toss the Nerf ball at them. In fact, they'll try to eat you no matter what you throw at them.

The different response to Nerf balls accounts for part of what happens with the other 90 percent of the visual signals that enter the human eye.

THE NEW PATHWAYS

The remaining 90 percent of the visual signal passes through a newer pathway along the lateral geniculate nucleus (LGN), our central "visual triage station" that sits across the front of the right and left lobes of the neocortex, the lumpy topside of the brain. The neocortex is the newest part of the human brain, originally appearing in mammals tens of millions of years ago and growing rapidly in humans only over the last million years or so. The neocortex is the part of our brain responsible for conscious thought, analytic decision making, naming, high-level processing—pretty much everything except basic survival (handled by the brain stem) and emotions (handled by the limbic brain, the layer between the reptilian brain and the neocortex).

After initial categorization in the LGN,

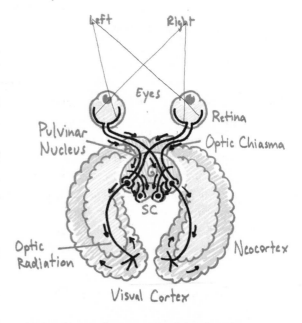

Ninety percent of incoming visual data flows from our eyes to our visual cortex via the LGN; 10 percent takes a different path via the SC (a fact that has interesting implications).

the visual signals pass through our optic radiation wiring channels to the primary visual cortex located at the back of the brain. There the impulses go through a more rigorous collating procedure where they are broken apart into two other pathways: the *what* pathway to the temporal lobes, where objects get recognized and identified, and the new *where* pathway to the parietal lobes, where more detailed information on position, location, and orientation of objects is processed.

Interestingly, this newer *where* pathway has been shown to serve as the visual guide for our motor system, which allows us to position ourselves, know where objects are in relation to us, and reach out and grab them. Because of this dual duty—telling us where objects are and guiding us as we spatially interact with them—this second pathway is also referred to as the *how* pathway.

From the *what* and *where/how* pathways, the visual signals are then passed on to any of thirty regions in the visual cortex where the really detailed processing takes place. From there . . . well, from there it's anybody's guess. So far, nobody really knows exactly what happens next. But from a visual thinking perspective—and this is what intrigues me— what we do know is that when we look at a scene, our vision system immediately breaks things down into distinct *where* and *what* information streams, each of which is initially processed independently. Then later, once the signals move into the higher processing centers of the brain, we can process the *how much,* the *when,* the *how,* and ultimately the *why.*

The point is this: It appears there *may* be a valid neurological reason why visually breaking a problem down into separate *who/what, how much, where,* and *when* components presents a powerful way of helping ourselves and others determine the *hows* and *whys.* It may simply be because that's one of the fundamental ways that our brains work.

How We See, Part 2: Right Brain Versus Left Brain

In chapter 6 when I introduced the SQVID, I pointed out that by asking the five questions, we force "both sides" of our brain into action. By now most people are familiar with the concept that the two hemispheres of our brains process information differently: The left hemisphere is *analytic,* piecing together small bits of data into linear, rational thoughts.

This left side contains the brain centers responsible for both written and verbal language and most mathematical calculation. The right hemisphere, on the other hand, is *synthetic*, processing large and less well-defined blocks of information through imagery, pattern, and spatial orientation. This right side has a higher propensity for addressing complexity and ambiguity and appears to contain the centers of creativity.

These distinctions first came to light in the early 1970s through the research of psychobiologist Roger W. Sperry and the "split-brain" operations performed by neurosurgeon Joseph Bogen. They reached popular culture mainly through the work of two women, one a writer and one an artist. Using Bogen's research as a starting point, Dr. Gabriele Rico wrote the landmark book *Writing the Natural Way,* which described how to take advantage of the creative tendencies of the right brain to assist the writing abilities of the left brain. Meanwhile, Dr. Betty Edwards wrote the classic *Drawing on the Right Side of the Brain,* which took a similar path and proposed that the act of drawing was a valid way for analytically inclined people to develop their creative abilities.

Both books quickly entered the public consciousness, and soon right-brain/left-brain analogies were applied to everything from understanding the arts to the actions of the stock market. To this day, the distinctions provide a powerful model for dividing problem solving into two main schools: businesspeople who look at the world according to a rational, quantitative perspective, and creative people who see the world in an emotional, qualitative way.

What I find most intriguing here is that vision processing appears to take place equally on both sides of the brain, possibly indicating that practicing visual thinking as I describe it here (active looking, seeing the 6 W's, using the SQVID, taking advantage of the <6><6> rule, etc.) activates both our analytic and creative capabilities in a way that neither speaking and writing nor drawing and doodling alone can match.

How We See, Part 3: The Things We Don't Know

By rights, this should be the longest section in this appendix. Reviewing textbooks on vision science and speaking with professors of neurology always leads to the same point: We have only begun to scratch the surface on understanding how vision works. That said, between the ongoing work of neuroscientists, physicians, cognitive psychologists, computer-vision researchers, artificial intelligence engineers, and specialists in countless other fields related to vision, our understanding is growing at an exponential rate.

In a way, the acid test of knowing whether we really "get" how we see will be when we can create machines that see as we do. In laboratories, research centers, universities, business parks, and garages everywhere, some of the smartest people in the world are working on such machines right now. I suspect that within just a few years we will have computers that can look at a scene and immediately see the *whos, whats, how muchs, wheres* and *whens*, then be able to draw their own conclusions about the *hows* and *whys* of the world as they "see" it. When that happens, I also suspect that the drawings they will make will look a lot like napkin sketches.

APPENDIX B

RESOURCES FOR VISUAL THINKERS

Software

I've made it a point throughout this book to emphasize the problem-solving power of a pen in hand. Notebooks, napkins, and whiteboards should be the tools of choice for those looking to improve their innate visual thinking skills. That said, the unbeatable processing, storage, editing, and communication benefits of computers ensure that most of us work almost exclusively on them today.

So until tablet PC's mature enough in both hardware and software to allow for spontaneous on-screen drawing, painless image manipulation and editing, and instant sharing with others, my best advice for the traveling visual thinker is to purchase either a midrange digital camera (any manufacturer) or even a portable flatbed scanner (good models are available from a handful of manufacturers, including Canon, HP, and others). With either device packed in your travel bag, you can draw on nearly anything anywhere, instantly record it digitally, and—using even the most basic image processing software—clean up, modify, annotate, save, print, e-mail, and present your pictures in minutes.

I wish I could also recommend pressure-sensitive digital drawing tablets as a good visual thinking tool, but I have used several and I personally find them to be more trouble than just carrying along a scanner. Unless you're going to be creating sophisticated painterly images, they have no advantage over paper and pen, but many disadvantages.

For those who must create the kinds of pictures described in this book using only software (and there are frequently compelling reasons to do so, especially when creating quantitative, data-heavy, or multilayered pictures), I suggest the following (in each case, arranged from the lowest learning curve for the average businessperson to the highest):

1. **Portraits:** Microsoft PowerPoint, Apple Keynote, Adobe Illustrator

2. **Charts:** Microsoft Excel, Microsoft PowerPoint, Apple Keynote, Adobe Illustrator

3. **Maps:** Mindjet, Microsoft PowerPoint, Apple Keynote, Microsoft Visio, Adobe Illustrator

4. **Timelines:** Microsoft PowerPoint, Microsoft Project, Graphus

5. **Flowcharts:** Mindjet, Microsoft Visio

6. **Multiple-variable plots:** Microsoft PowerPoint, Apple Keynote, Adobe Illustrator

Books

The following list of books serves as both a bibliography and a resource for those wishing to further explore visual thinking at the bookstore or library. These are all books that I found particularly inspiring and insightful while I was developing the ideas in this book.

CREATIVE PROBLEM SOLVING

Buzan, Tony. *The Mind Map Book: How to Use Radiant Thinking to Maximize Your Brain's Untapped Potential.* New York: Plume, 1996.

Degani, Asaf. *Taming HAL: Designing Interfaces Beyond 2001.* New York: Palgrave, 2004.

Gelb, Michael J. *How to Think Like Leonardo da Vinci; Seven Steps to Genius Every Day.* New York: Delacourte, 1998.

Grandin, Temple. *Thinking in Pictures: My Life with Autism.* New York: Vintage, 2006.

Kelley, Tom. *The Art of Innovation.* New York: Doubleday, 2000.

Root-Bernstein, Robert and Michele. *Sparks of Genius: The 13 Thinking Tools of the World's Most Creative People*. New York: Mariner Books, 1999.

Sawyer, R. Keith. *Explaining Creativity: The Science of Human Innovation*. Oxford: Oxford University Press, 2006.

Stafford, Tom, and Matt Webb. *Mind Hacks: Tips & Tools for Using Your Brain*. Sebastopol, CA: O'Reilly, 2005.

Thorpe, Scott. *How to Think Like Einstein: Simple Ways to Break the Rules and Discover Your Hidden Genius*. Naperville, IL: Sourcebooks, 2000.

Von Oech, Roger. *A Whack on the Side of the Head*. New York: Warner Books, 1983.

NEUROBIOLOGY AND VISION SCIENCE

Chalupa, Leo M., and John S. Werner. *The Visual Neurosciences*. Cambridge, MA: MIT Press, 2004.

Hawkins, Jeff, with Sandra Blakeslee. *On Intelligence*. New York: Times Books, 2004.

Palmer, Stephen E. *Vision Science: Photons to Phenomenology*. Cambridge, MA: MIT Press, 1999.

Ramachandran, V. S. and Sandra Blakeslee. *Phantoms in the Brain: Probing the Mysteries of the Human Mind*. New York: Harper Perennial, 1999.

VISUAL EXERCISES AND INSIGHTS FOR NONARTISTS (AND ARTISTS, TOO, OF COURSE!)

Arnheim, Rudolf. *Visual Thinking*. Berkeley: University of California Press, 1969.

DiSpezio, Michael A. *Visual Thinking Puzzles*. New York: Sterling, 1998.

Edwards, Betty. *The New Drawing on the Right Side of the Brain*. New York: Jeremy P. Tarcher, 1979.

Few, Stephen. *Show Me the Numbers: Designing Tables and Graphs to Enlighten*. Oakland, CA: Analytics Press, 2004.

Tufte, Edward R. *The Visual Display of Quantitative Information*. Cheshire, CT: Graphics Press, 1983.

Wainer, Howard. *Graphic Discovery: A Trout in the Milk and Other Visual Adventures*. Princeton, NJ: Princeton University Press, 2004.

Zelazny, Gene. *Say It with Charts: The Executive's Guide to Visual Communication.* New York: McGraw Hill, 2001.

OTHER NOTES ON SOURCES

The story on Orit Gadiesh and the origin of the Bain & Co. logo was inspired by the article "Orit Gadiesh, Consulting in the Right Direction," which appeared in *The Economist*, October 20, 2005.

The story on Herb Kelleher, Rollin King, and the Southwest Airlines napkin was inspired by information found on the Southwest Web site at http://www.southwest.com/programs_services/adopt/about_southwest.html.

INDEX